How to Sell CLOTHING, SHOES, AND ACCESSORIES on eBay

Other Entrepreneur Pocket Guides include

How to Sell Collectibles on eBay

How to Sell Toys and Hobbies on eBay

Start Your Real Estate Career

Start Your Restaurant Career

Entrepreneur MAGAZINE'S POCKET GUIDES

How to Sell CLOTHING, SHOES, AND ACCESSORIES on eBay

Entrepreneur Press and Charlene Davis

EP Entrepreneur. Press

Editorial Director: Jere L. Calmes
Cover Design: Beth Hansen-Winter
Production and Composition: Eliot House Productions

Library of Congress Cataloging-in-Publication Data

Davis, Charlene, 1957–
How to sell clothing, shoes, and accessories on eBay/by Entrepreneur Press & Charlene Davis.
p. cm.
ISBN-10: 1-59918-005-7 (alk. paper)
ISBN-13: 978-1-59918-005-2 (alk. paper)
1. Selling—Clothing. 2. eBay (Firm) 3. Internet auctions. I. Entrepreneur Press. II. Title.
HF5439.C6D38 2006
687.068'8—dc22 2006006681

Printed in Canada
12 11 10 09 08 07 06 10 9 8 7 6 5 4 3 2 1

Contents

Preface

Many people mistakenly think that eBay is like a giant online garage sale; however, nothing could be further from the truth. eBay is more than just a cool web site with neat stuff. The reality is that eBay is a large, lucrative community made up of millions of people from all over the world who are buying and selling products and services online. By virtue of eBay Marketplace's easy accessibility, buyers can look for affordable designer brands, custom-made accessories, hard-to-fit shoes and clothing, while sellers can leave their specialty shops open for business 24 hours a day, seven days a week.

More than 724,000 savvy entrepreneurs are making ends meet selling on eBay either as stand-alone businesses or to supplement their incomes. As fashion-conscious consumers greedily scour the internet for the best bargains, this is truly the best time to carve a niche in the Clothing, Shoes, and Accessories category.

eBay is continually evolving to accommodate the needs of its fast-growing community. It seems that less than a week goes by without it introducing a new feature or business partner. Some of the changes are subtle such as updating an obscure policy or revising a link. Other changes are more significant, like revamping the Sell Your Item form or adding a new subcategory. To stay informed, sellers should actively participate in the eBay community through discussion forums, workshops, and signing up for special announcements.

There are a number of responsibilities involved in selling apparel and accessories on eBay, and the purpose of this book is to help you streamline those tasks so that your business will run more smoothly and efficiently. We want to emphasize the importance of operating sensibly and ethically, while providing helpful tips and information about various tools to assist with improving your performance as a seller. Because security issues grow along with eBay's success, we will discuss how to protect yourself as an online trader and a consumer.

One of the neat things about running your own business is that you are the boss. The good news is that you get to make all of the decisions. The bad news is that you have to make all of the decisions. You also can't call in sick or defer someone to a higher authority. But there is no need to worry because we're going to help you get on top of your game with sage advice from successful eBay sellers, strategies to simplify your business structure, tips to improve your online selling experience, details about the clothing, shoes, and accessories industry, and much more.

Whether you are an eBay novice or experienced seller, this book will provide the information you need to build and grow your eBay business and get on the fast track to success. So relax, start reading, and explore all of the options that will show you how to profit from selling clothing, shoes, and accessories on eBay.

CHAPTER 1

Falling for **Fashion**

EVERYWHERE YOU LOOK YOU WILL SEE FASHION: ON THE street, in magazine ads, on prime-time TV, in newspapers, or featured on the sides of busses. The only way to avoid fashion is to walk around with a shopping bag over your head. Even then you will still be able to see the trendy footwear styles that are outpacing apparel sales across the nation.

Last year, Americans spent more than $177 billion on clothing, shoes, and accessories. This figure is up 2.2 percent from the previous year, according to the NPD Group, a Port Washington, New York, retail research company.

Name-brand labels reign supreme and have since the 19th century when designers like Charles Frederick Worth began to be viewed as artists instead of talented servants for the rich and famous. Hollywood celebrities and top models set the pace by sporting vogue apparel and accessories, as designers furiously compete with one another in the continually evolving fashion industry.

Consumers are finding new ways to stretch their dollars and have found they are not required to have deep pockets to look good and keep up with the "beautiful people." Shopping for clothes online offers a convenience that cannot be rivaled by retail stores, as shoppers are more likely to find styles, colors, and sizes that are agreeable with their wallets, as well as their finicky tastes and diverse shapes.

Thanks to online emporiums like eBay, fashion is more accessible to savvy shoppers. With over 1.5 million items listed in Clothing, Shoes, and Accessories, buyers can find everything from brand-new designer suits, to wholesale lots, to one-of-a-kind vintage clothing items. eBay provides a huge opportunity for knowledgeable sellers to offer affordable, trendy styles to outgoing women who want a bigger selection of modern maternity clothes, big and tall men who are frustrated with finding apparel that fits, and fashion-conscious children who outgrow their clothes faster than they can put them on.

Sellers need to know their customers—what they think, what they want, and what they will buy—so it's important to stay on top of current fashion trends. When it comes to the world of fashion, the one constant you can always count on is that it will change—sometimes overnight. Little lacy camisoles that were previously worn as innerwear under a sheer blouse are now donned as street wear paired with faded jeans or a Gucci suit.

In Category Tips found at eBay's Seller Central, readers can find out how successful sellers in the Clothing, Shoes, and Accessories category maximize sales and profits, while gaining a competitive edge by learning new tips and strategies. In addition, they can learn what the current best-selling items are, forecasted trends, how to gain an edge over the competition, as well as talk to other sellers about the best ways to polish and sharpen their entrepreneurial skills.

Learn the art of up-selling and cross-selling making direct pitches to shoppers by suggesting an accessory from your

TIP

At eBay Sellers Central look at "What's Hot" to find out what things in your category shoppers are screaming the loudest for. Or put your finger on the eBay Pulse to see what items buyers are watching and searching for the most often.

store that matches the skirt just purchased. This strategy is one of the least invasive and is basically the same as fast-food chains encouraging customers to "value-size" their combo meals. Include free or discounted shipping with your offer and you'll be able to scratch another item off the inventory list.

I hope you're excited about starting a business on eBay in the Clothing, Shoes, and Accessories category. I don't want you to become so jazzed that you'll make some crazy mistakes that could be costly ones, so please read every chapter in this book. Perhaps like some eBay sellers you are a shopper who needs to fund a habit, or you have bought so much stuff online that you now need to downsize. On the other hand, like many other sellers, you may have an entrepreneurial spirit and want to run a business doing something you enjoy on your own terms. Whatever your reasons, eBay is the perfect vehicle. It's exciting, pleasurable, profitable—and hard work—and you're going to love it!

CHAPTER 2

Smooth **Operators**

WITH EVERYTHING INVOLVED IN STARTING A BUSINESS ON eBay—considering what to sell, thinking of a User ID, and setting up your operation—we decided to go to the experts for advice. The successful eBay sellers interviewed for this book come from diverse backgrounds with an endless range of experience and goals. But they each share the seriousness with which they approach their respective businesses. They believe good customer service is a top priority, that everyone should have a niche or specialty, and they look forward to discovering and learning new things.

Meet the Sellers

Jennifer Koch (eBay User ID: thebridalcollection), whose eBay store is The Bridal Collection, started selling on eBay in 2003, when she decided to be a stay-at-home mom following the birth of her second child. "I was already an eBay shopper and thought I should be able to sell things easily enough," she says. "So I started listing my kids' used clothes and a few other things here and there, before branching out and selling denim wear purchased from a local wholesaler."

Things took a turn in a big way in 2004 when the owner of the bridal shop where Koch had previously worked as a manager, decided to close and sell off the store's remaining inventory on eBay. The bridal shop owner encouraged Koch to get into this niche and offered her some sample wedding dresses to sell online. From there, the bridal ball rapidly gained momentum and Koch became a PowerSeller within a few short months. "This is an area that I'm very knowledgeable about and had been in for years, so it was a great transition for me," she says.

Before she began selling on eBay in 2002, Karyn Michaels (eBay User ID: whattachloegirl) of Bucks County, Pennsylvania, had been a pharmaceutical representative whose job was phased out. Like many sellers, she started out on eBay by selling things she had around the house, including toys and baby items. The first auction she posted was her toddler's infant bedding set, which immediately set off a bidding frenzy because it was a discontinued pattern in big demand. As her business grew and evolved into the selling of new and used designer and boutique infant wear and children's clothing, Michaels achieved PowerSeller status six months later.

Because of her rapid growth, Michaels recently moved her business from home to a nearby combined office and warehouse big enough to accommodate all of her merchandise and supplies. The additional space also provides ample room for her five part-time employees to move comfortably around when setting up auctions to be listed or preparing items for packing and shipping. She attributes her eBay success to a career path born out of necessity. "I have a kid in college with a daughter right behind him, as well as a younger child with a disability," she says. "And I didn't want to be 'owned' by another company—especially at this stage in my life." Michaels feels being an eBay seller is a wonderful opportunity for anyone who has the desire and imagination to make it work. "You don't need a business degree to do this," she asserts. "That's the real beauty of it all."

Linda Ott-Albright (eBay User ID: shoppe*head2toe) of Pasadena, California, considers her eBay business selling new and used designer clothing for girls more of a fun diversion that allows her to earn extra cash. She initially began in 2003 by weeding through her daughters' clothes and things around the house. "I hate clutter," she says. "But with three kids, two cats, and a dog, you're always going to have it." In the past she had always donated or thrown away unwanted items, but after discovering that her trash was someone else's treasure she enthusiastically embarked on this new adventure.

"This all really started as a hobby," she laughs. "I didn't realize it had turned into a business that was financially beneficial until six months later when I became a Power Seller." Although Ott-Albright actively sells on eBay only six months out of the year, she is able to maintain her PowerSeller status year-round through sales from her Head-2-Toe-Shoppe eBay store. During the summer months and winter holidays she doesn't post traditional auctions, although her store is always open. This allows her to spend more quality time with her family.

When Stephanie Inge (eBay User ID: stephintexas) of Rowlett, Texas, first became interested in eBay in 1999, she was running an antique showroom at the World Trade Center in Dallas. Having just made her first eBay purchase, an inexpensive digital camera, she decided to put it to good use and auction off some of the items in her showroom. "I just got tired of everything collecting dust," she says. "So I started liquidating things online. Within a month we closed up the shop to sell exclusively on eBay."

As she ran out of collectibles to sell online, Inge looked around to see if there was a different area she should concentrate on and discovered that vintage cowboy boots and western wear were all the rage. It also helped that she lived in an area where she had access to a lot of quality merchandise in this niche.

While Inge was in the process of establishing herself as a top-notch PowerSeller, she started privately teaching individuals who also wanted to learn how to sell on eBay. In 2003, she decided to kick her teaching practice up a notch by offering classes through local community colleges and ultimately becoming an eBay Certified Education Specialist. "I wanted eBay's blessing, so I signed up, studied hard, and passed the test," Inge says. "Then I basically incorporated their curriculum into mine." She now instructs beginner and intermediate classes at six different college campuses.

In New Jersey, Amy Caraluzzo (eBay User ID: princess*dreams*boutique) stumbled upon eBay in April of 2003 without a clue as to what the site offered. Her first clothing purchase was an item from the popular children's Gymboree line and that was all it took to set the wheels in motion. Within two months she began selling custom-made accessories specifically designed to coordinate with children's designer and boutique brands. "Buyers love purchasing one-of-a-kind items," Caraluzzo says. "I offer quality products at good prices, plus I take custom orders which have enhanced my business."

Although her selling venture started out as a fun way to profit from her fabulous creations, things took a serious turn in 2004 when Caraluzzo's husband had a severe stroke. Their family dynamics changed overnight as she found herself in the new roles of a loving caregiver and business woman. Proceeds made from sales on eBay are now used to supplement the limited disability income her husband receives. "During the time my husband was in the hospital, I crocheted flip flops while traveling back and forth on the train," she recalls. "This was actually a therapeutic release for me during a difficult time. The recognition that my bows, flip flops, and embellished socks are now receiving, have made it all worthwhile."

As you read these sellers' start-up stories and glean helpful tips and tricks from them in the pages ahead, what comes through loud and clear is that selling on eBay is much more than just a means to an end. It's an enjoyable livelihood that enables people to control their destinies while earning comfortable livings or supplementing the family incomes. Countless mothers are able to stay home with their young children, while other parents help put older children through college. Retirees are plumping up their nest eggs alongside family members who are selling and saving for a special vacation. Lasting friendships and business alliances have been formed through eBay among members who socialize, strategize, and help one another.

So if you are looking for a full- or part-time business that can be done from the comfort of your home or in a commercial setting, you've found it. And if you are looking for anything more, you will most likely find that too.

What's In a Name?

Everything! Choose your eBay user ID thoughtfully. This is the name under which your reputation as a buyer and seller will be established. Consider the image it's likely to project to prospective customers and be sure that image matches the one you want to portray. If it's too weird or cutesy, buyers may sniff and turn away without taking the time to look at your great stuff. Make your user ID something that will be easy to remember. A combination of letters and numbers that might make perfect sense to you (say, the first two letters of each of your children's names, followed by their birth months) could be hard-to-remember gibberish to someone else.

The Princess*Dreams*Boutique was created by Caraluzzo because she feels that all little girls dream of being a princess. And her unusual, one-of-a-kind accessories help to fulfill that fantasy. Koch, who sells designer wedding dresses, felt it would be more professional if her user ID, store name, and e-mail address all consistently featured the same name: The Bridal Collection. "I just wanted everything to flow together," she says. Ott-Albright took a similar approach by combining her user ID (shoppe*head2toe) and store name because she wanted it to be easy to remember. And who could forget "stephintexas" Inge who sells the beautiful vintage cowboy boots?

Check to see if the user ID you have selected is available. You can do this for any name without committing yourself to using it by looking up user IDs with the Advanced Search feature. The search results will show exact matches, as well as IDs that closely resemble the one you typed in. If yours has already been chosen by another member, refer back to your list and think about how the name can be changed to still accurately reflect your specialty. For example if you wanted to sell designer handbags, "baglady" might be a catchy user ID. But after discovering this name has already been taken, think about clever variations such as "snazzybaggys," "lady-in-bags," or "bagdeals." Even "pursesnatcher" would be an attention getter, but the objectionable connotation might be a turn-off for buyers who are humor challenged.

It's not uncommon for sellers to make mistakes with their original user IDs and want to change them later, but they may be reluctant because they don't want their customers to lose track of them. However, buyers who have marked you as a "favorite seller" will have your new user ID automatically updated on their My eBay page. But if they haven't marked you accordingly, people who have done business with you

TIP

Visit Nameboy.com (www.nameboy.com) to find clever and interesting user IDs in your area of specialty. This is a great free nickname generator that can be used for finding names for almost anything, although it is primarily used to find domain names for web sites. Simply type in two keywords that best describe your business and let Nameboy do the rest.

before may not be able to find you by searching for your old user ID. Another drawback of changing your user ID is that you get a "name change" icon next to your new user ID for 30 days, and that could make some new potential buyers suspicious—especially if you have done it several times before. One good thing about changing your user ID is that Your history follows you, and your feedback remains intact, so any reputation you've worked hard to build will come with you no matter what your user ID is.

Finding Your Niche

Many eBay sellers start out by selling odds and ends they have around the house—a process that often leads spouses threatening to nail down items they don't want sold. But this is a good learning exercise *and* a great way to get rid of stuff that you'll never miss and you don't want to store or dust anymore. If those items are in good condition, you'll probably get more for them on eBay than by having a garage sale. And because these are items you already own, selling them on eBay is a virtually risk-free way to gain practical eBay experience.

Once you have finished cleaning out the basement and your children are back on speaking terms with you after selling off their toys, it will be time to seriously consider what niche you want to focus on. Choose a specialty area you are knowledgable about by reflecting on what skills, hobbies, or products you know the most about. Caraluzzo says that crafters have a gold mine right at their fingertips. "People love to buy one-of-a-kind items, especially for children," she adds. "Whether you sew it, knit it, or paint it, custom-made products have a high sell-through rate."

Koch recommends that people who want to start selling clothing and accessories on eBay find a specialty that is unique and different, preferably something with a brand-name. "You have to have a special niche," she advises. "Otherwise, you're going to get sucked into the thousands of items that are already on there."

If you are unsure about what specialty area you should focus on, start thinking about your niche by making a list of things that you have first-hand knowledge about. Include common items, as well as a combination of unusual or hard-to-find things. Next, do a traditional search on eBay for each listed item to see how many other similar products are for sale. Then look at the completed auctions to see what the

THE NICHE LIST

Factors to consider when deciding what to sell are:

- *Strengths*. Choose products that you know, have experience with, and are interested in. Are you a crafter who can make custom or personalized items such as clothing, accessories, or handbags? What are some of your favorite brand names? If you already have a business, take it to a new level by promoting those items on eBay.

- *Cost.* What kind of investment will you have to initially make for these items? How will you fund it? If you don't have available cash and have to borrow the money (with interest), it may be to your advantage to find a less expensive alternative, if only for a short time.
- *Packing and shipping.* How much will it cost to pack and ship the item to your customer? If something is fragile, bulky, or heavy, additional charges will be incurred that are generally passed on to the buyer—and they can be quite vocal about paying hefty shipping fees.
- *Storage*. Will you be able to adequately and safely store the product while waiting for it to be sold and shipped? Items should be kept out of harm's way so that nothing will be damaged in the interim.
- *Seasonal.* Some items will sell better at certain times of the year. For example, swimsuits are difficult to sell during the Christmas holidays, unless someone is planning a vacation to the Bahamas. However, if you have addressed the storage issue above, it can be quite profitable if you buy end-of-season merchandise at greatly reduced prices and hold it until it is ready to sell.
- *Life cycle*. If the product you have chosen is something wildly trendy that is selling like hotcakes today, be aware that tomorrow you may not be able to pay someone to take it off your hands. Remember stirrup pants?

final closing prices were for those items. If the market is not saturated, and the merchandise is fetching a fair price, you may have found your niche.

You can find out by listing a few auctions as a way to test the waters and see what kind of response you get. If the test drive doesn't turn out to be as successful as you had hoped, step back and take another look at your list to find some new potential markets.

Getting Into the Groove

Now that you've had the opportunity to think about what direction you want to take with your new business, let's talk about how to get started. If you are not already a registered user, that will be your first step. Signing up at eBay is pretty much a breeze as they will walk you through each step of the process. Hopefully you have completed the exercise outlined

TIP

As an added measure of security for buyers, eBay sellers can take the extra step of becoming "ID Verified." This can also be an alternative for users who do not want to place their credit card or bank account information on file with eBay.

above for selecting an appropriate User ID, because that will be your first step in the registration setup.

Immediately following your User ID you will need to choose a password that you—and only you—will have access to. You want to make it difficult for the hackers to crack the code, so use a combination of letters and numbers with at least eight characters or more. Although it will be simpler for you to remember, refrain from using easily identifiable information such as your children's or pet's names, family birthdates or anniversaries, or even your social security number. "Type in something randomly like four numbers and three letters," Karyn Michaels advises. She also urges folks to change their passwords regularly and not to use the same ones for other sites. "I know it's easier to have the same password for all of your accounts," she says. "But that's what these hackers are counting on. If they are able to decode your main password, they will be able to get into everything in one fell swoop."

The next thing you will want to decide is what types of payment forms you will accept. Caraluzzo only accepts PayPal because it's quick and easy, and offers the Seller's Protection Policy. Koch agrees that PayPal is everyone's preferred method of payment, although she accepts checks and money orders. "I've only had a couple of people in the last three years who sent me a personal check without any problems," she says. The different types of payment forms that can be used for eBay auctions are discussed in Chapter 12.

TIP

Build your feedback rating more quickly by shopping on eBay and paying for purchases with PayPal. This speeds up the transaction so the seller can ship your item faster. Or cut out the shipping process altogether by purchasing inexpensive digital products, such as ebooks.

Now that you are set up, it's time to get to work. If you are a new user, browse the eBay site and look at other auctions of interest. Take some of the tutorials and read the discussion boards that are found at eBay Community. Helpful members like Stephanie Inge are always happy to answer any questions that you may want to post. "I'm a huge fan of the eBay Community," Inge says. "Not only is it the first place I go to find answers, but as an educator, I also try to mentor others when I have extra time."

Before you start selling, make sure you are familiar with the process by becoming a buyer first. This will give you the opportunity to see how the process works, while building up your feedback rating. You don't need to make extravagant purchases and, chances are, you will find things that you would buy somewhere else anyway.

CHAPTER 3

Rolling and Scrolling **Through the Racks**

ONE OF THE EXCITING THINGS ABOUT LOOKING FOR THINGS to sell on eBay is that merchandise can be found almost anywhere. In this chapter, readers will be provided with resources, ideas, and insider tips on how and where to look for specific items to sell. If someone wants to sell "new-with-tags" clothing and accessories, they will learn how to approach vendors and manufacturers, as well as develop a sharp eye for seasonal items that have been significantly reduced. Sellers who specialize in vintage wear or other types of secondhand clothing will discover that after their closets have been emptied, garage sales and thrift shops are not the only reliable sources to find good bargains.

What's Hot

Start by taking a closer look at some of the areas of interest within the Clothing, Shoes, and Accessories category on eBay and the impact they have on the fashion industry:

Name Brands

Designer labels such as Prada, Coach, and Banana Republic have always been a runway hit in the world of fashion—whether it is new or used clothing, shoes, or accessories. And this doesn't just apply to adults. Today's teenagers are obsessed with name brands, although their wallets may not support their increasingly sophisticated tastes. Also, during recent years a number of high-end designers have introduced clothing lines specifically for babies and children. By targeting the younger generation, these savvy marketers are hoping to establish brand loyalty that will last through adulthood. Of course this

TIP

When it comes to children's clothing, gently used name brands such as Gap, Gymboree, Old Navy, Osh Kosh B'Gosh, or Carters (just to name a few) are always in high demand. They wash up extremely well and can be sold in "like new" condition.

passion for fashion can take its toll on bank accounts and credit cards, and that is where venues like eBay come in.

Brand-New with Tags

New clothing and accessories that are sporting original retail tags are always a big draw for eBay consumers because it has never been worn by anyone else. Also, new-with-tag (NWT) items don't have to be a name brand to be a hot item. Although some retailers are starting to get in on the action by auctioning their own store items, just remember that on eBay everyone is on a level playing field. There are many resources for finding NWT products, which we will discuss in more detail in this chapter.

Secondhand

Gently used clothing and accessories are a mainstay for eBay sellers and buyers alike. Items that are in good condition—preferably "like new"—can bring top dollar, especially in subcategories for children, maternity, special occasion, vintage, or if they feature designer labels. Make sure to check items for tears, stains, or other blemishes. If something has a ripped seam or missing button and is otherwise in good shape, patch it up to be resold for a higher profit.

Vintage

Vintage is one of the top areas on eBay. Vintage wear are fashions and accessories that are no longer made, hard to find, and in big demand. To familiarize yourself with vintage designs, study old magazines and patterns to see how they are constructed. Teach yourself how to recognize true vintage wear by analyzing its style, fabric, label, and the way it's sewn. Research successfully closed eBay auctions and join focus groups to network with industry professionals. Purchase vintage clothing pricing guides so that you can educate yourself on values. This will come in especially handy if you are getting ready to pass over a $20 dingy leather jacket that was made by the East West Musical Instruments Company in the 1960s and is now worth over $3,000.

Custom-Made

Handcrafted and personalized "boutique" items have always commanded a big presence on eBay because people love having things that are one-of-a-kind. Selling custom-made items can seem a bit daunting, but many crafters have found eBay to be a great source of revenue because of its huge audience. And even if you are not personally a crafty person, consider entering into a joint venture partnership with someone who is, and splitting the profits. Or you can purchase the items directly from the crafter and resell them on eBay, keeping the profits for yourself.

Finders Keepers

Now comes the fun part—looking for the merchandise you want to sell. Most eBay sellers agree that looking for new treasures is the best part of their job, which is why it often seems more like a hobby than a business.

Sample Sales

From clothing and accessories to shoes and handbags, sample sales are a great way to get designer goods at deep discounts. Lynda Ott-Albright (eBay User ID: shoppe*head2toe) lives in the Los Angeles Basin and frequently has the opportunity to visit manufacturers' sales at the L.A. Market Center to purchase items for her eBay store, the Head-2-Toe-Shoppe. "I have been very spoiled because of my access to the Market," she confesses. "It has been a great asset to my business."

Buying sample sales directly from the designers and manufacturers gives you an early peek for the upcoming season, as well as discounted bargains at 40 to 80 percent off retail prices. They are the shopping secret of the fashion conscious, as well as one of the best ways to get beautiful, authentic name-brand merchandise without paying full retail prices. They are also a good way to check out and purchase unique items from newly emerging designers who haven't yet hit their stride in the fashion scene.

Some designer sample sales require you to make an appointment or at least have your name placed on their guest list. But don't let this intimidate you as very few sales are limited to a specific audience. Simply call and let them know you are coming. While you have them on the phone be sure to get the exact address so you will know where to go. Sample sales are frequently held in office buildings and warehouses without the benefit of directional signs to guide you.

The best times to attend a sample sale can vary, but try to avoid the lunch crowd (11:00 A.M. to 2:00 P.M.) because that is when they are the most crowded. Early in the morning on the first day of the sale is always a good time because the best items will be displayed and easy to find. As time goes on, the items will become disorganized and picked over; however, they will usually be offered at even bigger discounts as the end of the sale approaches. Ott-Albright says that although the morning is definitely a good time to go, "When its nearing the end of the sale, I can pick up things way below wholesale because the vendors have to liquidate."

Because she is a regular attendee at many of the sample sales, Ott-Albright has developed an easy-going rapport with several of the wholesalers who now allow her to visit their showrooms on non-sample days. She adds, "I think it's very important to network with the vendors and build a friendly relationship because there can be special perks in it for you."

To find sample sales in your area, check the newspaper for listings of upcoming manufacturers' sales. Your favorite designers' web sites often have mailing lists that you can subscribe to for information on upcoming sales. Join focus groups to network and discover sample sales that will be held in your area.

Buying Wholesale Clothing from Manufacturers

Many high-volume eBay sellers purchase merchandise directly from wholesale sources to be resold on eBay. When it's done right, wholesale clothing can provide high profit margins along with high-volume sales. The hard part sometimes is weeding through the junk to find quality distributors, so you may have to get down in the trenches and do some digging.

Don't waste your money purchasing lists of wholesalers, when you can find them on the internet for free by typing "clothing," "wholesale," and "manufacturer" in your browser. And avoid distributors who charge administrative or setup fees. To refine and narrow your search for wholesale clothing manufacturers, look for specific designers. Most have web sites, but if they don't you can at least get their company's contact information and ask for a catalog and price sheet for retailers.

Sometimes local wholesale distributors will advertise in the Yellow Pages or trade publications. This is an added advantage because you can visit their showrooms and see the merchandise up close. Don't be shy about contacting manufacturers directly and asking for their overstock and closeout

TIP

You need to know the quality of the products you are buying before making a big investment, so don't hesitate to ask for samples if this is not a local company. Often manufacturers and wholesale distributors will provide samples of their merchandise for free, while others may charge a nominal fee.

deals. Smaller manufacturers don't always have a formal distribution center, but they need to move merchandise and will be happy to help you out in a win-win situation.

Not all wholesalers are created equal so you should familiarize yourself with each company's prices, shipping policies, warranties, and other terms of service. Depending on your niche, you may want to open accounts with several distributors so that you can shop for the lowest prices and take advantage of specials each one may have. Be sure to ask for and check references so that you talk to other resellers who are buying from these sources. In addition, check with the Better Business Bureau, industry associations, and state regulatory agencies that can verify claims, if any.

The checking process is a two-way street and legitimate wholesalers will also want information about you. You will need to provide them with a sales tax ID number, as well as any required business licenses for your location. If they do not ask for this information, then they are not genuine wholesalers; merely glorified discount retailers. Wholesale distributors do not sell their merchandise to the general public—only dealers, retailers, and resellers like you.

If you've wondered why wholesalers aren't selling their own products on eBay, it may help to know that some of them are. Although those companies are your competition and can sell the same products for significantly less, they generally don't because they want to protect the pricing of the products that are out there by keeping the profit margin elevated. If

CAN DROP-SHIPPERS MAKE THE DROP?

On the surface, drop-shipping sounds like a great plan: You collect the funds, pay the distributor a fee, and pocket the change. In addition, you don't have to worry about keeping inventory or shipping the merchandise. Drop-shipping is a long-standing business practice, and when all parties involved do what they're supposed to, it is successful. The distributor doesn't have to worry about the retail sales process, and you don't have to handle the merchandise.

However, as with wholesalers, the hard part is finding a good, reputable drop-shipper who will ship the requested items in a timely manner. Disreputable drop-shippers have been known to throw their clients under the bus leaving an ugly trail of angry buyers who didn't get what they were expecting—or didn't get anything at all. To make things worse, this unattractive scenario is reflected in the seller's feedback for everyone to see.

Your reputation is contingent on the drop-shippers' reliability, so make sure they have solid track records backed up with good references. Give a prospective drop-shipper a test drive by ordering a product and having it shipped to a friend's house. This will give you the opportunity to see how quickly the shipper responded and in what condition the item is delivered. If there is a problem with the item or the delivery, you will be able to see firsthand how it was handled.

When you have a good working relationship with a drop-shipper like the one Jennifer Koch (eBay User ID: thebridalcollection) sometimes uses for her wedding dresses at The Bridal Collection, this can be a great way to set up shop, much like having a warehouse full of employees working for you around the clock. Plus, they will provide stock photos and item descriptions to use in your auction listings. You can find clothing drop-shippers by searching the internet, networking with wholesalers who sometimes provide drop-shipping services, and looking in the reference section of your local library.

they were to flood the market with goods that are much cheaper than similar merchandise being sold, retailers and resellers would no longer buy from them. Most wholesale distributors usually prefer to sell to business owners like you because they can sell more items in larger quantities without having to focus on the intricacies of the retail market.

Speaking of "larger quantities," when you buy wholesale items directly from the manufacturer, you are going to be dealing in volume. For example, clothing items will be delivered in shipments of large garment boxes. Most wholesalers have a minimum amount they will sell, and the more products you purchase, the better your cost per item will be.

Before you make a wholesale purchase, be sure you have the room to receive and store the inventory.

Retail Stores

Watch for advertisements at local retail stores for big sales that are held at certain times of the year. Merchandise that goes on sale after the season has ended can reap some of the best deals—as much as 75 to 90 percent off retail prices in department stores and specialty shops. Although the selection of items will be limited, the savings will be remarkable. Savvy shoppers know to look for bathing suits and sandals in October, and wool sweaters and fur hats in April. Avoid fads that may have a short life span. Select classic, timeless items such as handbags, wallets, and clothing that will carry over several seasons without going out of style. You can also find great bargains at stores that are "going out of business."

Amy Caraluzzo (eBay User ID: princess*dreams*boutique) always looks for name-brand items at retail store sales and closeouts. "I sign up for email notifications from all of the major upscale stores such as Gymboree, Old Navy, and The Children's Place," she says. "They in turn let me know of upcoming sales." Caraluzzo also says that some of the stores send her coupons and other incentives for greater reductions on merchandise.

Discount Stores and Clothing Outlets

Often brand-name companies such as Polo, Gap, and Carters send their seconds or unsold inventory to the manufacturers' clothing outlets or other discount stores, such as Marshalls or TJ Maxx. You can discover some great deals marked down 50 to 75 percent or more. These garments and accessories are top-quality, brand-new merchandise with the tags still dangling on them, which is a big draw for eBay buyers. Talk to sales personnel and find out when their scheduled shipments are, as well as "Final Sale" days to get in on the best deals.

Karyn Michaels (eBay User ID: whattachloegirl) of DesignRKidz recommends that someone who wants to begin selling items in the Clothing, Shoes, and Accessories category starts with this type of venue to test the waters. "I think a new seller would be better served by buying ten miscellaneous pieces from a clothing outlet before investing in a huge chunk of wholesale inventory," she says. "It's like sitting down to a really big meal where your eyes are bigger than your stomach. Take little bites to start with so the elastic doesn't snap back on you."

Consignment Shops and Thrift Stores

Look for consignment shops that carry high-end merchandise, as well as quality thrift stores run by charitable organizations. Most shops handle their inventory in the mornings, so make it a point to stop by first thing to increase your chances of finding the best items. Stephanie Inge (eBay User ID: stephintexas) looks for her cowboys boots and vintage wear in a variety of places including thrift shops, garage sales, flea markets, and estate sales, and she advises eBay sellers to

TIP

All previously owned garments must be cleaned before they can be sold on eBay. The exception to this rule is used underwear, which is not permitted at all. Please see eBay's policy regarding used clothing at: http://pages.ebay.com/help/policies/used-clothing.html.

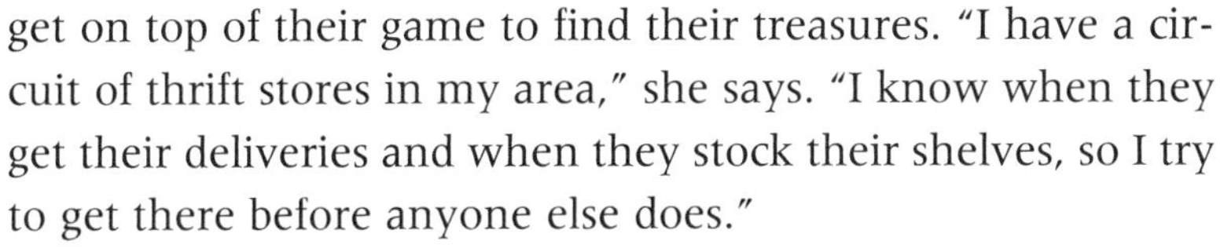

get on top of their game to find their treasures. "I have a circuit of thrift stores in my area," she says. "I know when they get their deliveries and when they stock their shelves, so I try to get there before anyone else does."

Many thrift stores have clearance days such as "Red Dot Wednesday," where everything is half-priced. Consignment shops also have traditional sales just as retail stores do, so get on their mailing lists or talk to sales personnel to find out when upcoming sales will be held.

Garage Sales

Garage sales are the backbone of eBay clothing resellers who have a specific niche and know what they are looking for. This gives you the opportunity to handpick specialty items for a small investment to be resold at a higher profit. Even crafters are able to find supplies at greatly reduced prices for their custom-made items.

Most garage sales are held on the weekends and you will be competing with other resellers, hobbyists, collectors, and frugal-minded folks, so use your time wisely. Sit down with the classified section of the newspaper and a map so that you can plan out a route that will include at least five to six garage and yard sales. Look for garage sales in affluent areas as they often have high-end, designer clothing and accessories. Community-wide garage sales are a huge bonus, and don't pass by unadvertised garage sales along the way.

Next, get your beauty sleep the night before because you will need to get a very early start. When you arrive at your destination, head straight for the clothes rack, children's table, handbags, display, or other main area of interest. Stay on target and don't get sidetracked by other items because you will have a lot of ground to cover in a short amount of time. You will find that as mid-morning rolls around the pickings get slimmer, so your mission is to "hit and run."

Before setting out, make sure you know what your spending budget is for the day and don't go over it. It may help to place the money in a separate envelope to be used specifically for that purpose. Garage sales are usually "cash only" transactions, so leave the checkbook and credit cards at home. Bring small bills ($1s and $5s), as well as a roll of quarters so the host or hostess will not have to worry about making change.

Develop friendly negotiating skills to see if sellers are willing to come down on their prices. One approach is to ask what

TIP

Stephanie Inge says that shoe repair shops are another source to find quality footwear. "Sometimes people forget to come back and get their boots or shoes and after a certain amount of time goes by, the shop will sell them nicely repaired and in good condition," she advises.

is the lowest amount they will take for a specific item. Another method is to simply offer a dollar amount based on what you are willing to pay. Always remain respectful, but be willing to walk away if the seller is not flexible.

To save time and keep things on track, make a list of items that you are specifically looking for such as name brands, sizes, colors, and so on. This will help you to remember to look for certain important items at each sale you go to. Also, remember to wear comfortable shoes and bring snacks, water, and sun block. If your children are escorting you on this adventure, be sure to pack some toys and goodies for them too.

Estate Sales

Estate sales are generally held when someone has passed away or is relocating to a smaller facility and needs to liquidate and dispose of belongings. They are more organized than a typical garage sale and are usually held inside a home or an auction warehouse. Estate sales that are handled by nonprofessionals such as family members generally yield better results for the reseller because the host may not be as savvy about resale values. But even when a professional is in charge of the sale it is certainly in your best interest to check it out.

Heirloom accessories, used designer clothing, and vintage wear are some of the wonderful treasures you can find at an estate sale. Clothing and shoes are usually displayed in the bedrooms, although coats, outerwear, and some accessories may be exhibited in other areas of the home.

Look up estates sales in the classified section of your local newspaper. Contact local auction houses in your area to see when they will host their next estate sale. You can even look on eBay for estate sale listings.

TIP

When visiting estate sales, garage sales, and flea markets, take a cloth tape measure with you. It comes in handy to measure items such as inseams, hems, sleeves, shoe heels, and straps on handbags. If you forget the tape measure, remember that a dollar bill is about six inches long.

Flea Markets

Flea markets may be another great source for finding clothing and accessories to resell on eBay. Just remember that the dealers are there to earn revenue, so you need to be sure that you can successfully resell the items for a profit. Go early in the morning to see the best selections. Take a quick tour before buying to see what different types of items are being offered. Many vendors have similar merchandise and competitive prices. You may also find hand-crafted, one-of-a-kind items that are in demand on eBay. Picking up a dozen custom-made belts to resell could bring in a generous profit.

Inspect the items carefully to make sure there are no stains, tears, or other flaws. Flea market goods are generally sold "as is" without the benefit of a return policy. To keep your hands free, bring along a small wagon or a cart on wheels to carry your things around as you do your shopping. Just as when you are at a garage sale, approach the vendor with a friendly manner to see if he or she is open to negotiations. Sometimes they will offer discounts if you are buying in quantity, but you will need to ask.

Flea markets are usually held under a roof and sometimes inside of a building. If the weather is nasty outside, this is the perfect time to go while others are staying at home. The vendors will be delighted to see you and will do their best to make you a deal you can't refuse. Another strategy is to go to a flea market late in the day when the dealers are tired and ready to unload their merchandise.

Become a Trading Assistant

Trading Assistants are experienced eBay sellers who sell items on eBay for people who, for whatever reason, don't want to do it themselves. There are plenty of people out there who have a closet full of things to sell, but are never going to take the time to post their items on eBay—and they're happy to pay a commission to someone who is willing to do it for them. These people can provide you with an endless source of items to sell.

As a Trading Assistant, you set up your own system for how you will deal with clients. You decide what services you'll provide, what types of merchandise you'll handle, the fees you'll charge, and all the other necessary terms. Trading Assistant Stephanie Inge (eBay User ID: stephintexas) specializes in vintage cowboy boots and western wear and charges a flat commission of 35 percent, which includes the auction and payment processing fees. "Its less paperwork for me and a lot easier to calculate," she says. In addition to the commission fee, her main requirement is that the items have a market value of $50 or more. Other potential fee structures for Trading Assistants include a flat or percentage listing fee in addition to the final value commission, whether or not the item sells.

eBay maintains a directory of Trading Assistants who have met the site's requirements. To qualify as a Trading Assistant, your eBay account must be in good standing, you must have sold at least four items within the past 30 days, and have a feedback score of 50 or higher with 97 percent or more being positive.

Consignment Selling

Whether you become an actual Trading Assistant or you just get good enough that people ask you to sell for them, you should understand the issues involved in consignment selling on eBay. Selling on consignment means the owner of the item asks you to handle the sale process and pays you for your efforts. When the item is sold and delivered, you deduct your fees and commission from the sale price and send your client a check for the remainder. Consignment fees can range from as low as 10 percent to as high as 40 percent or more.

TIP

Remember that eBay is a great resource to find items to sell on eBay. You can find plenty of wholesale lots that you can buy and then split up to be relisted individually. Also take advantage of the less than stellar listing practices of fellow eBayers. Look for misspellings in titles, or find auctions that have poor quality photographs or descriptions. These auctions will have very little, if any, bidding activity and you can purchase the items at bargain prices to be resold later.

Never accept anything on consignment without a written contract spelling out all of your terms and conditions.

Always take physical possession of items you are auctioning on consignment so that you can handle the shipping and everything else. Even though you are not the actual seller, your reputation as a seller will be at stake and this will help to prevent things from going wrong. For example, a seller may ask you to sell his or her grandmother's antique wedding dress and will promise to handle the shipping if you will take care of the eBay part. But if the seller doesn't ship, perhaps because she wasn't happy with the amount the item sold for, or if she ships but packages the dress so poorly that it arrives damaged, you're the one who will have to deal with the resulting customer service issues. Better to handle it yourself and know that it will be done right.

CHAPTER 4

Tailoring **Your Auctions**

TO PUT SOMETHING "UP FOR AUCTION" ON EBAY IS NOT complicated or difficult—however, it's not quite as simple as those three words might sound. The online auction world is not a one-size-fits-all proposition. eBay provides several auction formats for sellers to use and in this chapter we will discuss them in detail. As you're getting started, you may want to do some experimenting with the different types of eBay auctions to see how they work and how to use them to their best advantage in the Clothing, Shoes, and Accessories category.

Traditional Auctions

Traditional auctions are the backbone of eBay. They run for 1, 3, 5, 7, or 10 days. The auction begins with an opening bid and when the time is up, the highest bidder is the winner. This is a very easy process; however, depending on your business strategy and the type of product you are selling, you may want to think about using other types of auction formats. All of our sellers use traditional auctions, although they sometimes combine them with other formats mentioned below. In addition to her store's fixed-price listings, Lynda Ott-Albright (eBay User ID: shoppe*head2toe) uses traditional auctions approximately six months out of the year when she is actively promoting her eBay business. "I find that regular auctions have always worked much better than other formats," she says.

Reserve Price Auctions

Auctions that have a hidden minimum price are known as reserve price auctions. The reserve price is the lowest amount the seller is willing to accept for the item. Buyers are not shown what the reserve price is; they only see that there is a reserve price, and whether it has been met. If the reserve price is not met, the seller is not obligated to sell the item. To win the auction, a bidder must meet or exceed the reserve price and have the highest bid.

In a reserve price auction, bids are made as usual, but bidders receive a notice if their bids do not meet the reserve price.

Once the reserve is met, the item will sell to the highest bidder when the auction closes.

Sellers see reserve pricing as a way to protect their investments without revealing up front how much they want to get for items. You can also lose customers, as many bidders avoid reserve auctions because they can't tell what the lowest winning bid needs to be, and they don't want to waste their time bidding on an item that may have a high reserve figure. Amy Caraluzzo (eBay User ID: princess*dreams*boutique) says that when she has a high-priced item she will place a reserve on the auction so that the bidding can start lower and encourage more lookers to check it out. She adds, "I really don't like using reserves because they sometimes scare off buyers. And I rarely bid on a reserve auction myself, unless I absolutely have to have that item." The bottom line is to be discriminating when placing a reserve on an auction.

Buy It Now (BIN)

This is a feature you can add to a traditional auction format that gives bidders the option to bid on your product or to buy it immediately. With Buy It Now (BIN), you set the price you're willing to sell for, and bidders can either place a bid for less than that amount (but at or above your starting price) or win the auction instantly by paying the BIN amount. When a bidder agrees to the BIN price, the auction ends. If someone places a bid below the BIN price, the BIN option disappears.

A good strategy used by many sellers is to start the bidding at the absolute minimum you will accept for the item, then set the BIN amount close to full retail. Let's suppose you have a Kate Spade black handbag that you bought at a sample sale for $69 with a retail value of $180. You could start the bidding at $79 and offer a BIN of $150. If you get anything in between, you've made a profit and the customer is happy with his or her bargain.

Fixed Price Listings

Technically, a fixed price listing is not an auction because there is no bidding, but those listings show up in auction search results. This popular format allows users to buy and sell items immediately at a set price, with no bidding or waiting. You can sell more than one of an item in a fixed price listing, which saves you time and money in listing fees. For example, if you had a dozen identical wallets, you could list all of them in one swoop for the same sticker price. However, if you had purchased custom-made belts that were each different in design, you would need to list them in separate, individual auctions as eBay prohibits "choice listings." The exception to that rule is if you are the custom designer and were offering to design each belt to the buyers' specifications for the same price.

Private Auctions

In most auction formats, anyone looking at the item can see the user IDs of the people who are bidding on it. With the private

DUTCH TREAT

When a seller offers two or more identical items for sale in the same auction, it's known as a Dutch (or multiple item) auction, where you sell large quantities of a single item with just one listing.

When you post a Dutch auction, you decide on the minimum bid amount you're willing to accept and list that along with the total number of identical items you have available. Bidders specify the quantity they're interested in and the highest price they're willing to pay per item.

What makes Dutch auctions interesting—and complicated—is that all winning bidders pay the same price per item, which is the lowest successful bid. Most commonly, all buyers pay the starting price. But if there are more bids than items, the items will go to the earliest successful bids at the close of the auction. Bidders may bid on any quantity but have the right to refuse partial quantities.

Bidders in Dutch auctions do not receive outbid notices from eBay, nor can they use eBay's proxy bidding system (which allows a bidder to enter a hidden maximum bid), so they must actively monitor the auction and rebid if necessary. The most important things to keep in mind when using the Dutch auction format are that the items in a single Dutch auction must be absolutely identical like the wallets mentioned earlier, and the auction itself must be listed in the appropriate category. Don't be tempted to try something known as "Dutch avoidance"—that is, listing a single item and offering additional identical items for sale in the item description—the practice is dishonest and against eBay policy. Listings that violate this guideline will be terminated by eBay.

auction format, however, the bidders' user IDs are not seen on the item or bidding history screens. When the auction is over, only the seller and winning bidder are notified via e-mail.

This format is useful when you believe your prospective bidders may not want their identities disclosed to the general public. Well-known collectors often prefer private auctions. A common use of this format is when only the knowledge that a certain collector is bidding on an item would greatly increase the interest in the auction. Private auctions are also appropriate for items not intended for mass viewing, such as adult material.

Live Auctions

This particular type of auction is of more interest to an online buyer than a seller, but it's something you should know about. eBay's live auctions feature allows you to bid real time on auctions that are happening on the floor of offline auction events. You can place absentee bids, bid against the floor, or just watch people duke it out—all from the convenience of your home or office. For more information, go to www.ebaylive auctions.com.

Restricted-Access Auctions

Restricted-access auctions make it easy for buyers and sellers to find or avoid adult-only merchandise. To sell, view, and bid on adult-only items, users must have a credit card on file with eBay. Items listed in the adult-only category are not included on eBay's New Items page or the Hot Items section, nor are they available by any title search. Failure to list an adult-only item in the correct area could result in a suspension.

eBay's policies stipulate that all users must abide by all applicable regulations regarding the sale and distribution of adult materials, and any violation of the law is also a violation of eBay's user agreement, and will be treated accordingly.

Want It Now (WIN)

This is a type of classified ads section where buyers can post requests for specific items and sellers are able to respond with matching eBay listings. This free service enables sellers to expand their market by actively looking for buyers for items they have on hand. You can search by category or keywords. You can also save your searches to be used again and elect to receive alerts on corresponding Want It Now (WIN) requests. Perhaps a buyer is looking for psychedelic bunny slippers and you just happen to have a pair that has been sitting in your eBay store for a couple of months. Once you've determined that you have the matching item she's looking for, you can then send an e-mail to the buyer through eBay with a link to your listing. One out of two WIN bids results in a successful transaction.

Best Offer

As a seller you can choose to allow prospective buyers to make an offer on your listing; however, these auctions need to be set up as a fixed price format. Many buyers search specifically for auctions that have a "Submit Best Offer" feature, so this can be an additional marketing tool. Caraluzzo says that using this format has been very profitable for her business and helps her move inventory quickly. Once the offer has been made, you and the buyer can start your negotiations. Best Offers are binding and all messages relating to the transaction must be conducted through eBay and not violate any trading policies. Buyers are only allowed to make one offer per listing, so if you decline a bid, the buyer cannot come back and try to haggle with you. This is to encourage people to seriously make their best offers from the onset. You will receive an e-mail notifying you when a Best Offer has been made and you have 48 hours to respond before the offer expires, so check your messages often.

Become a Virtual Shopkeeper

Along with putting merchandise up for auction on eBay, you may want to consider opening an eBay store, which would allow you to sell your fixed price and auction items from a unique destination on eBay. eBay stores make it easy to cross-sell your inventory and build repeat business.

According to eBay, you should open an eBay store if you want all your listings displayed in one customizable place; if you want to be able to easily generate repeat business and encourage multiple purchases from the same buyers; if you want to control what you cross-sell to your customers; and if you want to maintain a larger permanent inventory than you can selling through auctions.

eBay stores offer a convenient selling platform for all your eBay listings—auctions, fixed price items, and store inventory. eBay promotes stores in several ways. All your auction listings will contain the eBay store icon; when bidders click on that icon, they are taken to your store. That icon is also attached to your eBay user ID for increased visibility. The eBay store directory is designed to promote all stores and will drive buyers to your particular store. You will also receive a personalized eBay store web site address that you can distribute and publicize as you wish.

The process of opening an eBay store is almost as simple as setting up your initial user ID. The only requirements are that you be a registered eBay seller and have a minimum feedback rating of 20 or be ID-verified. Any items that you have in active listings at the time you open your store will not appear in your store. But any auctions or fixed priced listings you post once your store is opened will automatically appear in your eBay store.

TIP

Store listings do not typically show up in regular keyword searches unless there are 20 items or less in the search results. Sellers need to regularly post traditional or fixed-price auctions to remain visible in the public eye.

eBay offers three store levels: basic, featured, and anchor. All have their own customizable storefronts and the ability to list store inventory, but featured and anchor stores include additional services. Here's how the three levels differ from one another:

1. *Basic.* Your store is automatically listed in the eBay stores Directory and will appear in every category directory where you have items listed.
2. *Featured.* Your store rotates through a special featured section on the eBay stores home page; receives priority placement in "related stores" on search and listings pages; and is featured within the category directory pages where you have items listed. In addition, you receive monthly reports on your sales and marketplace performance.
3. *Anchor.* In addition to the services offered to featured stores, your store can be showcased with your logo within the eBay stores Directory pages. It will also receive premium placement in "related stores" on search

and listings pages, which means your store will be placed higher on the page than the featured stores.

The cost of a basic eBay store is a nominal monthly fee (current rates can be found at www.ebay.com) that increases with the level of services you desire, along with additional fees for items listed and sold. Store inventory listings are less expensive than auction listings and appear for a longer period of time. Check eBay for current store subscription fees.

Setting Up Your Store

As with your user ID, you should choose the name of your store carefully so that it projects the image you want to portray to prospective customers. Typically, sellers select store names that closely correspond with their user IDs, including Stephanie Inge (eBay User ID: stephintexas) whose store is called Texas State of Mind and Ott-Albright who operates the Head 2 Toe Shoppe. Jennifer Koch (eBay User ID: thebridalcollection) decided it would makes things easier and more professional if her store name and user ID were the same.

You want to apply the same principles to stocking your eBay store as you would a bricks-and-mortar store. eBay allows you to create up to 20 custom categories for your products, similar to aisles in a physical store. You may decide to use product- or designer-based categories or you might use a more flexible system, with categories like "sale items," "bestsellers," and "seasonal." Clothing and shoes are also commonly categorized by size, style, or color to help shoppers quickly find what they are looking for. Consider having a category for new items so people who visit your store regularly can quickly see what you've added recently. These custom categories can be changed and updated as often as you wish, which is a significant benefit to a seller whose inventory changes frequently.

Your store site should also clearly explain how you operate. Take advantage of the Store Policies page to provide a complete and professional description of your policies and procedures. Use About My Store to establish your credentials and provide some history about you and your company. Make sure that each store listing incorporates the same features as a traditional auction with a good title, clear pictures, and adequate description.

Appearances really are everything and you want your store to look attractive and appealing so that customers will have a great shopping experience. eBay offers a nice selection of templates, graphics, and colors for store owners to use when setting up shop. Many store owners prefer to use their own templates or ones that have been obtained elsewhere. You can even purchase custom store templates on eBay.

Koch used PixClinix.com to professionally design her store, logo, and auction templates so that it would have the look and feel of a prestigious bridal store. A few months ago, Inside Edition decided to do a story about wedding dresses that were sold on eBay and chose her as one of its interviewees because they liked the classy, elegant look of her eBay store.

TIP

eBay Stores come with a powerful feature: Store newsletters. Use one of the promotion box tools to invite people to subscribe to your mailing list. You can then send out highly targeted emails promoting specials, sales, and other events happening in your store.

Use Your Store to Cross-Sell and Up-Sell

All eBay store subscriptions have the advantage of strategically placing promotion boxes in storefronts on different pages that can highlight featured items, provide special announcements, or be used in a variety of ways to showcase your store.

You also get cross-promotion tools that help you up-sell by allowing you to control which items your buyers see after they bid on or buy one of your items, or use the checkout function after a transaction has ended. You can choose different items to show on each listing.

The tools work by allowing you to establish "merchandising relationships" for the items you list; this determines which items the buyers will be shown. You determine what goes together by designating relationships for as many or as few items as you'd like. If you don't include cross-merchandise on one of your items, eBay will automatically select related items you are selling to display to your buyers.

Understand the Commitment

Your eBay store is open for business 24/7, whether you're awake or asleep. You need to monitor your store closely, answer questions from shoppers promptly, ship merchandise on schedule and as promised, and deal as soon as possible with any other customer service issues that might arise.

If you go on vacation or are going to be away from your store for any reason, you can either arrange for someone else to monitor the site and take care of your business or you can place your store "on vacation" with eBay for an indefinite period. However, you will continue to be charged the normal store subscription and listing fees.

CHAPTER 5

Getting Off to a Good Start

SETTING A GOOD STARTING PRICE IS ONE OF THE MOST important strategies a seller can use. If the price is too high, buyers will not be interested; if it's too low, a seller may take a loss; if it has a reserve, buyers may be reluctant to bid—and so it goes. This chapter will describe different tactics for determining a starting figure, how to set a Buy It Now price, when it's appropriate to place a reserve on an auction, and other strategies to induce buyers into a bidding frenzy. We will also discuss other starting points, including what category to place your listing in, the best times to launch and end an auction, and getting a jump start over the competition.

The Price Is Right

Your starting price is the lowest amount you're willing to accept for your item (unless you have specified a reserve price), and this is the amount at which bidding starts. Be reasonable when calculating this figure. Certainly you want to make a profit on what you sell, but sellers have found that setting the starting price too high often discourages bidding. A lower starting amount may attract a flurry of initial bidders who will quickly drive the price up. If you are using a fixed-price format, you'll enter a Buy It Now price.

Once you have a niche, you will be in a better position to develop a formula for determining starting prices, whereas if you are selling a menagerie of things, you may spend a lot more time trying to come up with different tactics. Jennifer Koch (eBay User ID: thebridalcollection) puts a lot of thought into deciding what prices to set for her wedding dresses. This process includes factoring in the retail price of the dress, how much she paid for it, and what kind of profit she thinks it will bring based on what the competition is doing.

Stephanie Inge (eBay User ID: stephintexas) tries to set her prices low enough to encourage early bidding, which creates a flurry of activity and drives the closing prices higher. "If you start the price low enough, people will go ahead and take the bait," she advises. "Once they see there are a couple of bids on the item, they'll wonder what is so great about those boots and click the link." Inge calls this the "empty restaurant syndrome." The way she explains it to her students is by telling them to imagine they are on vacation somewhere looking for a good place to eat. They come across two restaurants: one is a hole in the wall with a line of customers wrapped around the building, while across the street is a five-star restaurant without a soul in the parking lot. Which one would they choose? Nine times out of ten, people will go to the dive with all the people waiting to get inside because they want to see what all the fuss is about.

Lynda Ott-Albright (eBay User ID: shoppe*head2toe) takes a similar approach with setting low prices—often as little 99 cents. Her reasons are two fold: one is to encourage early bidding and the other is because the insertion fee is lower. Although this strategy usually works, she says it does come with risks. "I generally don't like to use reserves, but if I'm unsure about how well an item will sell I'll place a reserve on it for added protection," she says. "Then if that doesn't work I'll relist it with a higher starting bid." The 99-cent starting bid works best when you have a large potential market and will likely attract a large number of bidders, but if the item is not in high demand this strategy may not be the best one.

When to Use a Reserve Auction

As mentioned earlier, reserve auctions can be beneficial if you have an expensive item to sell but are hesitant to start the bidding too high. For example, let's say you came across a vintage pair of Persol 714 folding sunglasses like the ones made famous by Steve McQueen. These are easily worth $2,000, but you would do the happy dance if they sold for $1,500. If buyers see a starting bid that high they may keep browsing to see if they can find something less expensive. However a starting bid of $99 would definitely get their attention and entice them to click the link to your auction for more details. Of course, if the bidding doesn't reach your reserve of $1,500, you are not obligated to sell the sunglasses to anyone. However, if the final bid is close to your reserve you do have the option of accepting the bid and closing the deal.

Keep in mind that as we discussed in Chapter 4, buyers generally do not like auctions that have reserves placed on them because they can't tell what the minimum bid really is. Reserve auctions are a protective device for sellers who may have a high-priced item they don't want to risk a loss on by starting the bidding too low. But it's truly a risk either way because a buyer who decides not to play the "guess how much I want" game might have been willing to pay more than your asking price if they knew what it was up front.

Let's Buy It Right Now

Buyers like to have options and that is what a Buy It Now (BIN) gives them. For people who don't want to wait, this is a very attractive feature, especially during the holiday season when timing is of the utmost importance. The biggest downside for a seller using a BIN is that it puts a cap on how much they will get for the item by eliminating the possibility of a last-minute bidding frenzy. Amy Caraluzzo (eBay

TIP

Keep an eye on sellers who are selling the same or similar items that you are. If someone lists an auction with a Buy It Now option and you have a matching item, simply make your BIN $1 or $2 less. Both auctions will appear together in a search query but yours will be more appealing because it is less expensive.

User ID: princess*dreams*boutique) says that she uses BINs if she has a lot of inventory to sell because they typically bring in faster sales. Otherwise, she prefers to use a traditional auction and let the items bid up as high as bidders are willing to go.

If you are using a BIN option with a traditional auction format, one strategy is to set your starting price for the amount you would normally charge for a BIN, and set your BIN price a few dollars higher. The psychology behind this rationale is that unless the auction is closing in a few hours, buyers usually will snag the BIN option because the price is so reasonable and they can get the item faster.

Sellers—Start Your Listings

Timing is everything and if you are familiar with your customers' shopping habits, you can take advantage of them when scheduling your auctions. Listing and ending times for auctions, as well as the duration, are critical because you want as many eyes to see your listing as possible. Most bidding occurs in the last few hours of an auction, so make sure that time is when your customers are likely to be online. For example, if you are selling children's clothing, you may find that closing your auctions late on weeknights works well, because that is when busy mothers have put their kids in bed and have time to spend on the computer. You will also want to be mindful of time zones. If you have an auction closing at 10:00 P.M. PST, most folks on the East coast will be in Snoozeville because it will be 1:00 A.M. EST.

Seven-day auctions are generally the most popular because they give buyers ample opportunity to see the listings. Occasionally sellers may want their listings to extend over ten days to include two weekends, especially if big ticket items need more exposure. There are also advantages to using the one-, three-, and five-day listings depending on your market, the time of year (e.g., holidays) and what you're selling.

Koch feels that the best times to start and end her auctions are on Sunday nights because eBay traffic seems to be higher. "I think it may be because more people are home during that time and it's more convenient to browse and bid," she says. A few times she has inadvertently launched an auction in the morning and noticed a clear difference in the browsing and buying activity for that listing.

Caraluzzo generally prefers five-day auctions and tries to add new listings every day of the week. She adds, "I know some buyers who swear that auctions should never end on a weekend, but let's face it—people are online wanting to buy things every day of the week."

If you are really on top of your game you can extend the duration of a shorter auction listing without incurring additional fees. Sometimes if a seller has a three- or five-day auction and there has been no activity, they will extend the listing time for two more days. Here comes the tricky part: because eBay will not let you make any changes to your auction in the final 12 hours, you must make the change prior to the cutoff time.

Fridays are generally the worst day of the week to end an auction because people are gearing up for the weekend. Also, people who take three-day weekends are usually away from their computers on Fridays and Saturdays. Experiment with

TIP

Amy Caraluzzo recommends using a calendar to remember the best times of the year to list seasonal auctions. A good rule of thumb is to follow the lead of retail stores—when they set out their holiday displays, upload your holiday auctions. If they promote swimsuits in March or winter coats in August—that will be a good time to post similar auctions.

different timing strategies to determine what will work best for you.

Choose the Right Category

Although many bidders shop for specific items by keywords, many others browse by categories hoping something will catch their eye. eBay will suggest categories for you when you list your item, but you can also browse eBay to find items that are similar to what you want to sell, and see what categories they're listed in. Check completed auctions and look for trends that indicate that listing an item in one particular category gets better results than another. Listing in the wrong category could be a big mistake.

Get a Jump Start on the Competition

Research completed auctions by looking at how successful sellers have set up their auctions. See what categories they listed their items in, if they used a BIN or reserve, how they described the garment, what types of pictures were used, starting and shipping prices, and so on. Inge says in the beginning she consistently researched completed items for boots that were comparable to the ones she was selling. Because her specialty is vintage cowboy boots, she rarely found an exact match, but she could look for certain styles and similar types of leather to get an idea of where to start.

Caraluzzo also searches through completed auctions as a guideline when setting up auctions. In addition to observing

CATEGORIES

Top levels for eBay's Clothing, Shoes, and Accessories category:

- Infants & Toddlers
- Boys
- Girls
- Men's Accessories
- Men's Clothing
- Men's Shoes
- Uniforms
- Wedding Apparel
- Women's Accessories, Handbags
- Women's Clothing
- Women's Shoes
- Vintage
- Wholesale, Large & Small Lots

Within the top levels, Clothing, Shoes, and Accessories has more than 1,000 subcategories and sometimes your item will fit into more than one category. For a small fee you can have your listing appear in a second category that will help increase its exposure.

starting prices, she looks to see if the duration of a particular auction was three, five, or seven days. She also thinks it's important to know what day of the week the auction started and ended on, as well as the time of day—morning or evening.

DO YOUR HOMEWORK!

Use the Advanced Search feature to look at completed auctions that closed with winning bids. You can do this by entering the appropriate keywords to find your competitors' auctions. Then check the box for Completed Listings Only, ask it to sort by "Price: highest first," and look for listings with a bold green dollar amount (red means the item didn't sell).

Although eBay only provides information on closed auctions for two weeks, if you have found a couple of sellers whose previous auctions you would like to see, click on their feedback and you will be able to pull up links to those auctions for up to 90 days. Details you should look for in *successfully* completed auctions are:

- *Starting price*. Look for the starting bid, as well as whether a BIN or reserve was used.
- *Listing times*. Take note of what day and time the auction started and ended. This could be a big clue as to the best times to run your auctions.

- *Titles*. A title should read like a headline. Look for a pattern of descriptive keywords used to draw attention.
- *Descriptions*. Again, look for descriptive keywords, as well as what type of information the seller includes in the description. Style and punctuation are equally important.
- *Eye appeal*. Look at the overall layout of the auction page. Is the seller using a template or other bells and whistles to attract attention?
- *Pictures*. First, check to see if the seller used a gallery picture. Next, look to see how many pictures are on the auction page, different angles used, and the quality of the photos.
- *Shipping*. Look closely at the shipping and handling rate to see if you can beat it.

CHAPTER 6

Measuring Up **to a Good Fit**

SHOPPING ONLINE FOR CLOTHING, SHOES, AND ACCESSORIES is often considered risky because the buyer is not able to try on the garments and footwear or inspect the accessories up close. A conscientious seller can help alleviate doubts by providing detailed listings with clear photographs and precise measurements. You also need to understand the importance of writing a clever title with specific keywords to draw attention to your auction, as well as learn about keyword spamming and brand-name misuse.

Stylish Headliners

What's in a name? Quite a bit when it comes to writing attention-grabbing auction titles. eBay allows 55 characters (letters and spaces) for your listing's title; make each one count. Your title must make a prospective bidder want to learn more about your auction. Amy Caraluzzo (eBay User ID: princess*dreams*boutique) says that she always makes a point of using specific keywords in her titles she thinks people will search for. Jennifer Koch (eBay User ID: thebridalcollection) also feels very confident in knowing what brides-to-be will type in their search queries.

It helps if your headline is clever and catchy, but above all, it must be accurate and factual. Misleading titles are against eBay policy and could result in eBay ending your auction early. Though you might see them often, devices such as "L@@K" and excessive exclamation points waste precious space and don't attract additional bidders because they are not looking for those terms. Use all capital letters sparingly and only to make certain words stand out.

With more than 80 million searches conducted on eBay every day, you have to think about how buyers will find you. Your title needs to include the keywords that someone who is looking for your item might conduct a search for. If you have room, include a related word so your listing will come up in more searches. Be creative in the language you use in your titles. Although misspellings are the kiss of death, grammar can be sacrificed for the sake of squeezing in additional keywords.

Think of everything your item relates to, and figure out how you might be able to get as many of those words as possible into your title.

Your title should also indicate why your listing is so special. If you are selling a brand-name item, include the brand in the title. If the item is clothing or something that comes in different sizes, indicate the size or color. This is an example of a good title from the men's clothing category:

BRUNO MAGLI Grey Zip Leather Jacket Mens, 40 R $1,300

Prospective buyers know at first glance exactly what this auction is about. It tells viewers this is a men's jacket with a

TIP

In the book I co-wrote with Jacquelyn Lynn, *Make BIG Profits on eBay: Start Your Own Million $ Business* (Entrepreneur Press, 2005), we devote an entire chapter to shopping on eBay. Although Chapter 2 was written for buyers, it is also very useful for sellers because it explains how customers can search for auctions using different keyword strategies, how sniping works, looking out for inflated shipping costs, and what to do if a seller fails to perform. Copies of this top-selling book are available in local bookstores and on Amazon.com.

zipper and includes the name of the designer in capital letters, the color, the size, the material, and the value. Now that you know how to write a snappy effective title, its time to work on penning irresistible descriptions.

Make a Fashion Statement with a Good Description

A well-crafted description gives bidders the information they need to make a buying decision, as well as demonstrates that you are a professional, conscientious seller—plus it will pay off in the price you receive. Your description should include:

- the name of the item;
- what the item is made of;
- when and where it was made;
- who made it (designer, manufacturer, etc.);
- what condition it's in;
- weight, size, and/or dimensions;
- notable features or markings; and
- any special background or history.

Everything in your description should be true and accurate. Don't say something vague such as "easily restored" if an item is damaged or missing buttons or anything else. If possible, identify exactly what needs to be replaced or suggest the buyer purchase the item to be used as parts for another piece. Caraluzzo advises sellers to be honest if the item is not in perfect condition. "Don't surprise your buyer with that little hole in the sweater," she says. Be sure to describe any snags, tears, stains, and other imperfections.

MEASURING UP

In the fashion industry, there are no standards for tag sizes and manufacturers are all over the map when it comes to their sizing regimens. Since buyers are not able to try on their garments in a fitting room, you will need to do the next best thing which is to provide detailed information about the item that includes exact measurements. Lay the garment flat on a surface and use a measuring tape for the following areas:

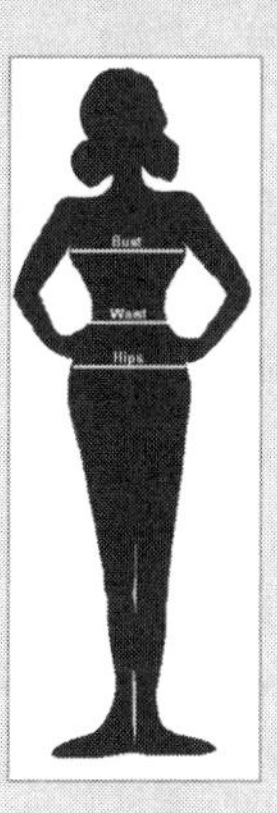

Bust. Measure from one armpit to the other and then double that figure to get an all around measure (e.g., 26 inches across the bust multiplied by two equals 52 inches).

Waist. Measure at the waistline and double for an all-around measurement.

Hips. Measure across the hips (approximately ten inches below the waist) and double.

Also include garment measurements for the length (shoulder to hem), inseam, and sleeves.

You might also add a personal touch to your description; many sellers have found that doing so can increase bids and sales. For example, specifically say what you like about the item, who it would appeal to and why, or how it could be used. If you know an interesting story about the item, share it.

One of eBay's most infamous auctions made history with a record-breaking 17 million hits featuring a burly, tattooed guitar player modeling his ex-wife's wedding dress. The best part of the auction was the description where he gave a wacky, satirical tale that revealed his sour grapes over the situation. Not only did the auction successfully close with a final bid of $3,850 (after a starting bid of $1), but the seller also received five marriage proposals, along with a book contract, a new web site, and a guest spot on NBC's *Today Show*.

Keywords Are the Key to Success

At least 80 percent of online buyers use basic search functions when looking for items and that includes browsers who are shopping around on eBay. For this reason, appropriate keywords are critical for both the auction title and description. If your competitors have not hidden their counters, you can watch their auctions to see which ones are receiving a lot of hits. This will be a good indicator that specific keywords have been inserted to draw in potential customers, so carefully examine their titles and listings to see which keywords or phrases stand out. Some sellers have invested in traffic analyzers to quickly and efficiently pick out strategic keywords, but if you have the time, you can do it for free while picking up some extra tips along the way. Then test applicable keywords in your own auction and see if traffic increases.

Avoid something known as "keyword spamming"—including words in your description that are not actually related to your item just because you think buyers would find those words appealing and because they are words a search would pick up. This is against eBay's listing policies.

eBay has also added a new section to its Keyword Spam policy that addresses "compatibility." Sometimes sellers use brand names to indicate their item is compatible with the product of a specific designer, which can cause confusion about who the manufacturer truly is. The update to the policy states (in part): "Sellers may not mislead buyers into believing they could be purchasing a product made by the same company that makes the brand or model with which compatibility is claimed." To avoid confusion, sellers are recommended to include words such as "compatible with" or "fits" in the title and description.

For more information on Keyword Spamming, visit Rules for Sellers in the Help section at eBay.

Use as many legitimate searchable words and phrases in your description as possible to be sure your item will come up when bidders are searching. For example, someone who is trying to sell a basic white blouse is simply going to cough up listing fees without anyone looking at it. Even if it's new-with-tags, there is a high likelihood it will get lost in the crowd of

5,000 other white blouses that are up for auction unless it has a coveted designer label such as Chanel or Escada. Instead, determine what is unique about that particular blouse. Could it be classified as vintage wear that is no longer made? Does it have special embroidery or lace, or perhaps look like a design worn by a celebrity? Let browsers know if the blouse can be paired with a square dance skirt or worn under a sarong.

You can also use your description to add details about shipping costs, payment terms, and any other details you think may be of interest to a bidder. Even if you plan to charge actual shipping, it's always a good idea to include at least an estimate of the shipping costs so bidders aren't surprised when the auction is over. Also, let bidders know if there are any restrictions on where you will ship, such as U.S. only, U.S. and

TIP

Knowing exactly what your customers are looking for can help you write better titles and descriptions so they can find your auctions. For keyword brainstorming ideas you can use Overture's free keyword suggestion tool found at: http://inventory.overture.com/d/searchinventory/suggestion/. Keywords are ranked in order of popularity giving you a better idea of what types of searches people are conducting.

Canada only, or to certain international locations. eBay has a shipping calculator that you can insert in your auctions that allows the buyer to determine how much it will cost to send that specific item to his or her address via United States Postal Service (USPS) or United Parcel Service (UPS). When you're finished, proofread and spell check—and then proofread again.

Sending Great Pictures Down the Runway

Placing clear, detailed photographs in an auction listing is a key element and important selling factor. Without them, your chances of selling the item are much slimmer because buyers are unable to "touch and feel" the items. Therefore, you need to appeal to their five senses by enabling them to see the articles through the eye of your camera.

Whenever possible, use natural lighting in lieu of a flash for a softer effect. Place the item against a plain, solid, light-colored background such as a wall or area draped with a sheet. Although one picture is sometimes enough, more is better. Stephanie Inge's (eBay User ID: stephintexas) auctions usually have six to eight photographs of her cowboy boots that include pictures of the heels, soles, inside, different positions, and any imperfections. "If there is a defect, take a close-up picture of it," she advises. "This goes along with good customer service and full disclosure."

Provide shots of different angles, as well as close-ups of buttons, designs, or textured fabric. Show off the shape of a long sleeve or lift a flared skirt hem slightly by attaching a long thread and securing the end to another point (or ask someone to hold it). Often you will see this trick applied in store window displays. Browse catalogs and look at their photos while thinking about how to apply those principles to your own setup.

Clothing generally sells better when photographed on a live model or mannequin versus dangling from a hanger, because the buyer has a better idea of how the item fits. With the exception of children's clothing, garments look dull when laid flat on a table or bed because the viewer is not able to see how the material drapes. There are a variety of different styles of mannequins and dress forms that can be found at reduced prices on eBay.

Koch uses a few stock photos from the manufacturer's collection, although she primarily uses pictures that she either has done by a professional photographer or takes in her basement. When she has professional studio pictures taken of a dress, she uses a live model who collects a modeling fee. Pictures that are taken in her basement are done by placing the dress on a black mannequin against a black background. This gives the dress the illusion that it is standing up completely on its own. "The white dresses against a black background are a nice contrast," she says. "Plus you can see the details more clearly without any other distractions."

Your pictures should also be free of clutter. For instance, if you are taking pictures of a handbag make sure that it is the only item on the table or desk corner. Just like the background, the surface of the area you are photographing should be

MAKE YOUR PICTURES WORTH MORE THAN 1,000 WORDS

A photo, indicated by a camera icon in your listing, will make a tremendous difference in the success of your auctions. Quality photos not only let bidders see what your product really looks like, but they also say that you're a serious, professional eBay seller. Use these tips to produce quality photos:

- Create a photo area in your home or shop with good lighting and a background screen for an uncluttered background.
- Consider developing a photo background with a distinctive color, pattern, logo, or company name that helps brand your business.
- If appropriate, showcase your item with accessories to display it to its best advantage. Be sure to indicate whether those accessories are included in the auction, are available separately, or are not for sale.
- If you sell clothing or jewelry, invest in used mannequins to properly display them. A box draped with a piece of plain fabric works as a display pedestal.
- Maintain a database of pictures so it's easy to pull up images for listings when you are selling items you've sold before.

- Invest in a quality digital camera.
- If you have a scanner, you can use print film and then scan your photos.

Once you have the pictures uploaded to your computer, you can then use a program or software to adjust and enhance your images.

plain. You don't want anything that will distract from the item being displayed. If necessary, cover the surface with a plain sheet or a piece of soft, velvety material. You can also crop out unnecessary background and clutter by using graphic editing software. Most digital cameras come with software that enables you to lighten, brighten, and enhance pictures. The appendix also lists a few online web sites to assist you with your photos.

Smaller accessories can sometimes be difficult to photograph, especially when you want to capture intricate details such as filigree, tiny clasps, or engraving. Even smooth gold or silver can look tarnished if the lighting is not reflected accurately. To do this successfully, place the item on a solid-colored background, such as a piece of navy velvet or maroon silk material. Next, surround the item with a light tent to provide diffused lighting. Light tents can be bought inexpensively on eBay or you can make your own by cutting a small hole in a large white bowl, container, or storage bin that is big enough for the camera eye to shoot down into. When displaying accessories such a hair bows or sunglasses, use a life-size Barbie styling head available in most toy stores—and of course on eBay.

CHAPTER 7

It's a Pleasure—Customer Service

GOOD CUSTOMER SERVICE IS ESSENTIAL FOR AN EBAY seller to be successful. In addition to understanding eBay's feedback program, sellers should learn how to establish a refund and return policy in case something doesn't fit or the color is wrong, how to deal with difficult or nonpaying customers, and how to effectively communicate with buyers so the transaction will have a happy ending.

Say It with a Smile

Do you sometimes—or even often—feel that good customer service is a thing of the past? It may be in some business environments, but eBay is a different story. eBay customers demand—and enjoy—a high level of customer service, and if you're going to succeed in selling on eBay, you need to take care of your buyers. Most of them know what they're looking for and have a good sense of its value, and they expect good service as part of the bargain.

What's different about customer service when you're selling on eBay? It's often more intense, with bidders asking a lot of questions and wanting fast answers. And because each eBay seller has his own policies and procedures, it's not uncommon for customers to become confused. When they do, it's your job to tactfully clarify whatever is at question.

Stephanie Inge (eBay User ID: stephintexas) believes that in addition to quality products and honest descriptions, providing great customer service gives her an edge over the competition. "I'm after a lifetime customer and I offer the ultimate in customer service," she says. "It's never an issue of who is right or wrong, because I'm going to make everything right for customers so they will keep coming back again and again."

An aspect unique to online auctions is the feedback system, where both buyers and sellers can leave comments about one another that are visible to all other eBay users. Providing poor customer service puts you at risk of negative feedback, which could have a serious impact on your sales. Though most eBay users are reasonable and honest with the way they use the feedback system, a few see it more as a weapon than a tool by threatening to leave negative feedback if they don't get the goods or services they want, regardless of whether their request is realistic. This attitude is referred to as "feedback extortion" and eBay has a firm policy against it that can result in the user's account being suspended. Naturally you should try to work with difficult customers as best you can, but don't let nasty customers intimidate you with the threat of negative feedback. Just remember that if a buyer leaves you negative feedback, the eBay system allows you to post a response to it.

Some customers are difficult because that's their nature—but others may give you a hard time simply because they don't know any better. eBay is one of the easiest ways to buy something on the internet, which means it attracts a lot of novice online shoppers. Sometimes their own insecurity and unfamiliarity with the process will make these "newbies" challenging to deal with. Rookie eBayers can sometimes be a nuisance, but remember that you were new once upon a time too. Sometimes new members may need a little hand holding, but think of it as an opportunity. If you take the time to nurture their eBay learning experience and guide them through the process, they (and their friends) may become loyal customers. That's why communication immediately following the close of an auction and then throughout the remainder of the time it takes to process the sale is critical. Try not to take it personally when customers are rude and excessively demanding. Not every transaction is going to go smoothly. The important thing to remember is to remain cool, calm, and professional.

Deadbeat Bidders

Unfortunately, deadbeat bidders are a way of eBay life. They are also another reason for clearly stating your payment terms in each auction description. Although they will try, it makes it hard for them to plead ignorance about your stated policies when they're in plain view. If a bidder doesn't pay in the time you stipulate in your terms and does not respond to payment reminders, you are free to relist the item or make a second chance offer to the next bidder in line. In either case, be sure to leave appropriate feedback and file a nonpaying bidder alert with eBay to receive a credit on your final value fee. You should also place a nonpaying bidder on your blocked bidder list so that you don't have to deal with that person again.

Communication Is Key

As soon as an auction closes, send the winning bidder a notice that outlines how the transaction will proceed. If you need to calculate the shipping before he pays, do so promptly. Let him know when you receive his payment and when you plan to ship. Once you have shipped, let him know the package is on the way and provide tracking information if available. Tell him when you post feedback, and ask him to post feedback for you when he has received the product. If you don't hear from him after he has had time to examine the item, follow up with an e-mail asking if he is satisfied. If he leaves you positive feedback, thank him and tell him you hope to do business with him again.

TIP

From the minute you post an auction, be prepared to respond to e-mails promptly. Remember, these are messages coming from potential or existing customers who may purchase again.

If you see a pattern in the types of questions you get asked, look for ways to answer them in your item description or on your About Me page. You can also develop standard responses that you can easily paste into an e-mail and quickly customize for the particular situation.

Treat all your communications with other eBay users as business correspondence, and remember that the structure, tone, and details of your e-mails are a strong reflection of your operation. Begin your e-mails with a salutation, write in complete sentences, end with a proper closing, and proofread and spell check; then proofread again before you hit "send."

Will You Take Returns?

Customer returns are inevitable, even for the most conscientious sellers. Buying online is a gamble and buyers will feel more reassured if they have the option of returning the item under certain circumstances. Decide how you're going to deal

HOW TO PROVIDE GREAT CUSTOMER SERVICE

Whether your business consists exclusively of auctions, or you also sell from a web site or even a brick-and-mortar store, the basic principles of customer service remain the same:

- *See your business through your customers' eyes*. Is your operation user-friendly, efficient, and responsive?
- *Ask what your customers want and need*. Don't assume that you know what your customers want; ask them, and listen to their answers.
- *Meet or exceed expectations*. When you promise to do something—whether it's to provide information, ship a product, or something else—do as you promised, or better.
- *Ask if there's anything else you can do*. When the transaction is complete, find out if you can provide any other product or service. A simple, "Is there anything else I can help you with?" can net you additional sales and invaluable goodwill.
- *Keep in touch*. Let your customers know that they are important to you after the sale is complete and you have received their payment.
- *Be a copycat*. Pay attention to good customer service when you receive it, whether it's in a restaurant, the grocery store, or elsewhere, and duplicate those techniques in your own operation.

with returns and state that policy clearly in all your auctions. If your return policy requires in-depth explanation, provide this on your About Me page and refer to it in your item description.

Jennifer Koch (eBay User ID: thebridalcollection) believes that her return policy is very attractive to prospective buyers and helps boost her sales. "Most brick-and-mortar bridal salons will not allow a wedding dress to be returned, so the fact an eBay seller will is a really big deal," she says. Buyers have three days to contact her and let her know if something is wrong after they receive the dress. This gives them enough time to try it on a few times and see how it is going to work. "Planning a wedding and selecting a dress is very nerve-wracking," Koch says. "So having the option to return a big ticket item eases some of the pressure. And very rarely do I get a return."

Your return policy should include a time limit, a description of the circumstances under which items can be returned, who pays for shipping (Will you refund shipping costs if an item is returned? Most sellers don't.), whether you charge a restocking fee, and any procedures customers must follow to return an item. If your return policy promises to make refunds to dissatisfied customers, you are required by federal law to do that.

SquareTrade

SquareTrade is a great eBay tool to reduce the risk of problems with transactions. By displaying the SquareTrade seal on your auctions, you are demonstrating a level of trustworthiness, and buyers will feel confident that they will have a positive experience dealing with you. For a small monthly fee, SquareTrade offers buyer protection services, negative feedback notification, dispute resolution, and more.

SquareTrade also offers a sidebar that interacts as a shopping assistant by providing competitive price comparisons on eBay, as well as other online sites. This tool also includes anti-phishing and fraud detection technology by alerting users if they click a suspicious link. For additional information, check out eBay's SquareTrade section by clicking on the Services link at the top of eBay's home page, and then clicking on Buying & Selling.

Handling Feedback

Feedback is the tool by which an eBay user's reputation is built and is a large part of an eBay seller's success. eBay users leave 2.7 billion (and growing) feedback comments annually. There are three types of feedback—positive, neutral, and negative—and both parties in a transaction are encouraged to leave feedback about each other. For example, as a seller, you might leave feedback about how quickly a buyer paid; as a buyer, you might leave comments about how well the seller answered questions or how promptly the merchandise was shipped. Only the seller and the winning bidder can leave feedback about a particular transaction.

An eBay user's feedback rating is the number in parentheses after his or her user ID. The feedback rating is calculated by giving one point for each positive comment, no points for

TIP

What you write in feedback becomes a permanent part of that user's record on eBay, so use caution and good judgment, especially before leaving negative comments. You cannot change feedback once it has been posted. Only under rare circumstances, such as a mutual withdrawal agreement, will eBay remove feedback after it is left.

a neutral comment, and subtracting one point for each negative comment. You should always check a user's profile for negative feedback, whether you're buying or selling.

Don't automatically refuse to deal with an eBay user who has a few negative feedback comments. Consider the ratio of negative feedback to positive feedback. If a user has hundreds of transactions on his record, don't let two negative remarks dissuade you from doing business with that person. Also, look at when the negative feedback was left—recently or a long time ago? Read the feedback and get a sense of whether it was justified or not, or possibly retaliatory because the eBay member may have left negative feedback for that person. Many negative feedback comments sellers receive are in retaliation for negative feedback the sellers leave for nonpaying bidders. So be sure to read all negative feedback comments and decide for yourself if they're valid.

If someone leaves you negative feedback, you will be able to respond to the comments—and you should so that others can see your side of the story. Just remember that this will be a matter of public record so keep your response simple and factual, while remaining calm and professional. Something to the effect of "This is retaliatory feedback" or "Buyer refused refund," might be sufficient.

Although you are limited to 80 characters when leaving feedback comments, they should be thoughtfully written. Leave out the triple A's followed by 20 plus signs because they don't tell viewers anything about the transaction. Let others know if the buyer was responsive to e-mails or paid quickly by writing "Great communications" or "Prompt payment." Even something simple like "A pleasure to deal with," lets people know this was an easy transaction. You should leave feedback within 90 days of the completion of a transaction. Of course, the sooner, the better. As you're building your own eBay reputation, you'll gain a special appreciation for users who leave prompt feedback.

Common Auction Scams

Though it's not specifically a customer service issue, you should still understand the common scams that occur in the auction world, be able to recognize them, and know what to do if you believe it's happening in one of your auctions. Though eBay works hard to maintain the integrity of the auction process, unscrupulous people will always try to circumvent the rules to increase their profits. All the following scams are against eBay policies.

Bid Shielding

Bid shielding is when someone uses a secondary user ID or has another eBay member bid on an item to raise the bidding to an extremely high level, and then that high bid is retracted at the last minute, and the low bid level of another bidder is protected. An example would look like this: Mary puts a 1920s vintage flapper dress up for auction; the dress is reasonably worth $90. Susan bids $50 and then asks Kathy to bid $100 to scare away other bidders. Kathy places her bid but at the last minute retracts it. Because no one else has bid, Susan gets the dress at her bid of $50. eBay's proxy bidding system and policies on bid retractions make bid shielding difficult, but enterprising scammers will still try to do it.

TIP

Visit eBay's Security & Resolution Center (http://pages.ebay.com/securitycenter/) for more tips and information on how to protect you and your computer, the latest on auction scams, and how to become a trusted eBay seller.

Shill Bidding

Shill bidding has plagued legitimate auctions since they began in ancient Rome. In a traditional auction, a person known as a shill will place bids to drive up the price of an item and then back off and let another bidder win the auction when the price is sufficiently high. The same thing can happen in an online auction; someone places bids to artificially raise the price of an item.

eBay users might participate in shill bidding, either in an effort to generate interest in their own auction or to help a friend. Don't do this type of insincere bidding; it could result in being suspended from eBay. To avoid even the appearance of being involved in shill bidding, eBay recommends that family members, friends, and individuals who live together, work together, or share a computer not bid on each other's items. Even though eBay benefits from shill bidding because higher sale prices mean higher final value fees, buyers will be reluctant to bid if they suspect shill bidding, and that is ultimately not good for eBay as a company or the entire online auction community. In addition to being against eBay's policies, shill bidding is illegal in many jurisdictions and can result in criminal prosecution.

False Testimonials

Some sellers have been known to create fake user IDs so they can place glowing testimonials about themselves in the feedback section of eBay and in the comment sections of other auction sites.

This type of feedback shilling can also work in reverse if an eBay member wants to damage another user's account by leaving negative feedback. In addition to being unethical, this type of activity is fraudulent.

Counterfeit Money Orders

Another type of scam is when the seller receives a legitimate-looking money order in the amount requested and sends out the item before depositing the money order, only to discover later that the bank will not honor it because it's a fake. The best course of action is to cash the money order and then wait a few extra days before mailing out the item.

Another scam along the same line is when the buyer sends you a fake money order in an amount much larger than the winning bid. The buyer asks you to send the item and remaining balance to their friend or family member at another address (usually in a foreign country and impossible to recover). By the time the bank notifies you of the problem, you have already deposited the money order and sent out the product and monies as instructed. This means you lose the item, shipping costs, and hard-earned cash. If you ever receive a money order like this, immediately notify eBay's security team who will help you take appropriate action. The bottom line is to always confirm that you are in receipt of the actual funds before shipping merchandise.

CHAPTER 8

Laying the **Groundwork**

A STRONG APPEAL OF SELLING ON EBAY AND ELSEWHERE online is the low cost and flexibility of operating in a virtual world. But if you sell merchandise, whether you operate from the comfort of your own home or run your business from a commercial location, you need a place to store your merchandise, you need to track your inventory, and you need the right equipment to set up shop.

There's No Place Like Work

If eBay is going to be your primary sales channel, the process of selecting a location will be simple: you just need a place that has room enough for your inventory and can handle your shipping. You can choose to work from home or operate from a commercial/industrial facility, depending on your business operation.

Where to Set Up Shop

eBay has made it possible for more than 724,000 people to start profitable part- and full-time homebased businesses. A homebased eBay business can successfully function in a relatively small space, or it can take up a lot of room, depending on the merchandise you are selling. Amy Caraluzzo (eBay User ID: princess*dreams*boutique) says that she is fortunate to have a large unfinished basement to operate out of. "I'm able to keep my sewing machine, printer, scale, camera, and all of my storage bins in one convenient place."

First, you need a place to set up your desk and computer. You'll also need an area for staging product photographs, room for packing and shipping, and storage for your inventory and supplies.

It's ideal if you can set aside a room (or rooms) exclusively for business use. If you can't, do the best you can with the resources and room you have. Remember that to take the home office deduction on your taxes, the IRS requires that you have a room that is used solely for business. If you're only using part of a room, or if your office doubles as a den or guest room, a home office deduction probably wouldn't survive an IRS audit. You can, of course, deduct all other allowable business expenses.

An alternative to being completely homebased is to work from home but rent warehouse space for inventory storage and perhaps your shipping operation as Stephanie Inge (eBay User ID: stephintexas) does. "I keep all of my merchandise in a rented storage unit, but my main operation is conducted from home where I have a large office," she says.

If being homebased isn't part of your plan, consider a warehouse or light industrial facility. Or you may start from home then move as your business grows and you need more space as Karyn Michaels (eBay User ID: whattachloegirl) recently did when her eBay business outgrew her home basement. "We now have an office where I have three computers up and running, along with a small warehouse to store all of our merchandise and supplies," she says. "We also have an area that we use for packing and shipping the orders."

Also, keep in mind that the environment should be appropriate for your products. If your merchandise is temperature sensitive, make sure you use an air-conditioned facility. It should be dry, free of insects and other pests, and free of household odors such as cigarette smoke and pets.

Wherever you choose to locate, find out what sort of licenses and permits you need before you sign a lease or, if you're going to be homebased, before you start selling. Also, remember that commercial leases are far more complicated than residential leases. Make sure you completely understand what you're signing.

STAMP OF APPROVAL

If you are buying wholesale items to resell, you will need to obtain a sales tax ID number (sometimes referred to as a reseller's permit) which legitimate suppliers will want to see. This saves you from having to pay sales tax, while authorizing you to charge and collect sales tax when applicable, depending on your state's regulations. This is usually a simple process and you can check with your state's Department of Revenue for information on how to proceed.

Though used interchangeably, a business license is not the same as a reseller's permit, although you may have to obtain one before you can apply for a sales tax ID number. To make matters even more complicated, you may need more than one business license to operate, depending on where you live. Different states, counties, and cities have different regulations pertaining to these issues so you are encouraged to contact your state's Department of Revenue, the local city hall, and your county's business development division for more information.

The Small Business Administration is also great resource for small business issues. Of course, it's always recommended that you speak with a lawyer or accountant about compliance within your city and state.

Adequate insurance is also a consideration; sit down with an insurance agent who is familiar with your type of business, analyze your potential risks and exposures, then purchase appropriate and sufficient coverage.

Where to Stuff Your Stuff

Unless you use a drop-shipper, you need space to securely store your products. How much space you need depends, of course, on what you're selling and the amount of inventory you keep on hand. It's also helpful if your storage area is roomy enough to function as a packing and shipping station. Inge has her large office set up like an assembly area. "When the merchandise comes out of my storage unit, it comes here to be photographed and then it goes on a separate set of shelves," she says. "When its sold, I take it down and bring it over to the packing and shipping area to get it ready to go." Inventory storage options are listed in the following sections.

Space in Your Home

If you are homebased and your merchandise doesn't take up a lot of room, you may have adequate storage space in your home. If you are unable to use a basement or garage, designate a large closet or a room for your products. Keep seasonal items in marked boxes or bins until it's time to bring them out; garments that are ready to be auctioned can hang on racks.

Jennifer Koch (eBay User ID: thebridalcollection) is able to store her wedding dresses in a large room located in her basement. Some of the sample dresses that have been displayed by the manufacturer in trade shows and other events are sent to her on hangers and need to be packaged when they are sold. But others come to her already wrapped and ready for shipment. "Those are the ones I love to sell because they are a piece of cake," she laughs.

Self-Storage Facilities

Stephanie Inge will tell you that self-storage is a great option for a homebased business that needs a little extra space. You can rent space equivalent to anything from a large closet to an extra garage at a self-storage facility. Many offer options ranging from air-conditioned space, indoor access, loading docks, and more. Some operators will accept deliveries on your behalf if you can't be there to sign for them yourself.

Commercial Warehouse Space

If you maintain a sizeable inventory and your items tend to be heavy, you may need a commercial warehouse facility with a shipping dock. You'll find this type of commercial space in industrial (light and heavy) parks and mixed-use commercial areas. Some offer only warehouse space; others have small offices and even showrooms adjacent to the warehouse.

Public (Commercial) Storage

A viable option to your own commercial space is a public warehouse. Public warehousing companies can essentially function as your shipping department. In addition to storage, their services include pick and pack operations, packaging, labeling, and they will arrange for shipping on the carrier you specify. Public warehousing prices are based on usage—you only pay for the space and labor you use. Contract warehousing is similar in terms of services, but you pay fees whether or not you use space and services. Find public warehouse companies in your local telephone directory or through an internet search.

Remember that the more storage space you have, the easier it is to purchase off-season inventory that you hold until the time is right to sell. However, always remember to calculate storage costs into your cost of selling those items.

Whatever space you have designated for storage needs to be properly equipped and functional. You'll likely need sturdy shelves for boxes or bins, rods for hanging clothing, and a table to use for packing and labeling. Assign specific areas for items "to be listed," "listed," "sold, waiting for payment," and "ready to pack and ship."

Keep Track of Your Stuff

At any given moment, you need to know what you have on hand, what you've purchased that's on the way, what you need to buy, what's up for auction, what's available in your eBay store and on your website, what has been sold, and what has been shipped.

For small, low-volume sellers, a simple index card or file folder system will be sufficient. Another alternative is using a spreadsheet like the one created by Cathi Aiello of Allegro Accounting, Inc. (www.allegroaccounting.com). An active eBay seller and Trading Assistant, as well as a full-time bookkeeper, Aiello saw a need for eBay sellers to simplify their inventory tracking system and created a series of auction accounting spreadsheets to help streamline that process.

Many eBay sellers track this information electronically by using auction management software packages that include inventory tracking. Whatever inventory tracking system you use should tell you what's selling well—and what isn't. When items have overstayed their welcome in your home or warehouse, be creative about moving them out, even if you take a loss. For example, if you have an accessory that isn't selling well, group it with another accessory or clothing item and sell them together with a low starting bid. The idea is to free up storage space and bring in cash for new merchandise.

TIP

In our book, *Make BIG Profits on eBay: Start Your Own Million $ Business* (Entrepreneur Press, 2005), Jacquelyn Lynn and I walk you through the intricate steps of starting and managing your eBay business, including the need for a business plan, choosing a legal structure, and establishing policies and procedures for your operation.

Equipping Your Business with the Right Stuff

Most eBay clothing sellers start their businesses with equipment and inventory they already own, and you'll probably do the same. That's what makes eBay such an attractive business proposition. Even though you can get started with just your computer and a digital camera, there are other types of equipment and supplies that range from beneficial to essential, depending on your business needs. Some examples are:

- *Computer*. A computer is vital if you're going to be selling on eBay. And with the right software it can help you manage complex bookkeeping and inventory control tasks, maintain customer records, create a web site, and produce marketing materials.
- *Modem*. This goes along with the computer because modems are essential to access the internet. Another consideration is whether to invest in a cable modem or DSL for faster, more efficient operations.
- *Postage scale*. A postage scale is a valuable investment for eBay sellers because it takes the guesswork out of calculating postage, and will quickly pay for itself.
- *Digital camera*. Besides your computer, a digital camera is the most important piece of equipment for an eBay seller. As a bonus, most digital cameras come with photo editing software to enhance your pictures. Of course you can use a traditional film camera, but you will spend extra time and money on processing and scanning.

- *Storage bins.* Stackable bins are convenient for storing merchandise until it is ready to be sold. Be sure to clearly label what is inside so that you can quickly find what you need when you need it.
- *Garment racks.* If you sell clothing, using a garment rack can be a space saver while keeping clothes wrinkle-free. They come in all different shapes and sizes including racks that are wall-mounted, have wheels for portability, or other special features.
- *Boxes.* Sturdy, corrugated boxes that can withstand the test of time and travel can be purchased individually, in bulk, or collected from retail and grocery stores.
- *Padded mailers.* Cushioned envelopes are commonly used by eBay clothing sellers because they're lightweight and convenient for smaller garments and accessories.
- *Packing materials.* Bubble wrap, packing peanuts, tissue paper, mailing labels, and sealing tape are some of the essential materials you may need to adequately package your items.
- *Mannequin.* Using a mannequin or dress form to model clothing helps buyers to see how the garment drapes. They come in a variety of styles, shapes, and sizes to attractively display clothing and accessories.
- *Display tables.* As with mannequins, display tables come in different shapes and sizes that are easily transportable or can be installed as a permanent fixture.

- *Shelving*. Most eBay sellers will tell you that having shelves installed on the wall of your home office, closet, or warehouse is essential to keeping merchandise organized and within easy reach. You can also purchase storage shelves on wheels or a shelving unit that comes as one large piece of furniture.

CHAPTER 9

The Trader's **Toolkit**

IT'S EASY TO GET SET UP AS AN EBAY CLOTHING AND accessories seller; however, it will take a bit more work to build a substantial, profitable business with eBay as your selling platform. To create a professional online image that inspires confidence in buyers while streamlining your business, online shopkeepers should arm themselves with helpful, reliable tools. When it comes to auction tools, there are a surprising amount of choices: some free, some for a fee, some are offered through eBay, while others are third-party options. The following sections provide a brief rundown on some of the useful tools.

Cool Tools from eBay

eBay provides users with a variety of tools to enhance their auctions, and is constantly improving those tools and developing new ones. The goal is to make your eBay business as efficient and profitable as possible. Karyn Michaels (eBay User ID: whattachloegirl) thinks that eBay's tools are better today than they have ever been. "Their tools educate you before you even really get started," she says. "Plus they have wonderful tutorials at eBay."

My eBay

My eBay is the central hub where you can track and manage all your eBay buying, selling, messaging, account information, preferences, and more, and is available to all registered eBay users free of charge. Sellers can use My eBay to monitor current auctions as well as those scheduled to be launched, invoice buyers, print shipping labels, make a second chance offer, sell a similar item, relist an unsold item, and more. For small- to medium-volume sellers, My eBay will efficiently manage your operation from listing to leaving feedback.

Turbo Lister

Turbo Lister is a free tool popular among eBay sellers for many reasons: it's faster and easier to use than eBay's Sell Your Item form when preparing multiple auctions; it's rich in features for medium- to high-volume sellers; it creates auction listings in bulk; and it provides free, easy-to-use HTML templates.

Turbo Lister also allows sellers to schedule when auctions should be launched and make bulk edits to multiple listings at one time. Because this program is downloaded to your computer, you can work offline and upload the listings at your convenience. Another reason many sellers prefer Turbo Lister is that whenever eBay has changes, they can be easily integrated into the program so that you are always up to speed with current updates.

Blackthorne

Blackthorne is a program previously known as the Seller's Assistant and is also a downloadable program. Like Turbo Lister, you can do everything in bulk, including listing, launching, editing, and even posting feedback. It has sales tracking capabilities and will export sales data to your accounting program. Unlike Turbo Lister, this program is fee-based and has two versions: Basic and Pro (with more bells and whistles).

Selling Manager and Selling Manager Pro

Selling Manager is an organizational tool accessible through My eBay and is available for a small monthly subscription fee, except for eBay store owners who automatically receive the basic version for free. Selling Manager helps to keep track of your auctions once they have been listed, as well as advise you of post-closing activities that need to be completed. There are customized templates for e-mail and feedback, and you can print shipping labels and send invoices with just a click.

In addition to the Basic version, there is also a Pro version for high-volume sellers that helps manage inventory, provides selling statistics, and offers free designer templates. This program can be combined with Turbo Lister for optimum results.

Picture Manager

Picture Manager is a fully integrated online picture hosting service that subscribers can access from Turbo Lister, My eBay, the Sell Your Item form, and Selling Manager Pro without having to leave the eBay site. The monthly subscription fee includes tons of storage space for photos, the capability to add additional pictures to listings at no extra charge, and the ability to compress pictures to optimal eBay size. As added security you can protect your pictures by watermarking them with your User ID.

TIP

Confused by all the choices on eBay? That's understandable—and it's why eBay has created the Tools Wizard to help you decide what tools are most appropriate for your type of business. The Wizard takes you through a series of questions, then suggests one or more tools and provides a link for more information. Go to Seller Tools, then click on Tool Recommenda-tions to find the Tools Wizard.

Accounting Assistant

eBay sellers will have an easier time exporting their eBay and PayPal transaction data to QuickBooks by using eBay's Accounting Assistant. This free downloadable program is only available to subscribers of Blackthorne, Selling Manager, and eBay Stores. This can be a timesaver for medium- to high-volume sellers, as it helps to minimize time spent on data entry.

Third-Party Options

eBay's impressive growth has spawned a substantial market for third-party software and other online auction management tools. Some can be purchased outright, others are available for a monthly subscription fee, and still others are free for the taking. You'll find many third-party products listed in eBay's Solutions directory, or you can search the internet to find providers. Third-party software is particularly useful if you'll be selling on auction sites other than eBay. The following sections provide a sample of what's available to help you manage your online business.

Andale (www.andale.com)

Andale offers a range of research, auction, store, and management tools at competitive prices. They have exclusive technology relationships with eBay and PayPal, and provide integrated sales solutions for subscribers. Some of Andale's tools services include image hosting, templates, bulk listing tools, and free counters. They also have auction management tools to automate and manage your listings, including accounting, inventory, e-mail communications, and a payment processing system. And if that's not enough, Andale also can provide research reports so that you can quickly discover what's hot and what's not, what the best pricing strategies are, and the best listing times. This tool can even help you find the best products.

Market Works (www.marketworks.com)

Formerly known as Auction Works, Market Works is a leading provider of comprehensive online marketplace management software and services. They manage more eBay listings than any other third-party provider. This program is for the high-volume seller who is operating on more than one venue and needs an all-inclusive, fully automated organizational system for inventory, processing orders, checkout, sales reporting, and customer management. In addition, they will provide you with your own storefront to give you a bigger presence on the web.

ViewTracker™ (www.sellathon.com)

ViewTracker is a popular tracking software that tells you exactly how your auction visitors found you, what keywords they searched for, what categories they browsed, how they sorted their search results, if they're watching your auction, if they're planning a snipe, and more. Stephanie Inge (eBay User ID: stephintexas) is a big fan of ViewTracker because she can also tell how long someone has spent looking at her auctions, as well as how many times they came back to visit.

Vendio (www.vendio.com)

Vendio is a sharp contender in the auction management world and provides many of the same services as its competitor, Andale, including bulk listing software, image hosting, inventory management, checkout solutions, and sales performance reports. They also have free custom templates to give seller's auctions a professional look. Probably one of the best features is the Vendio flash-based gallery which provides scrolling pictures of all of a user's auctions within individual listing descriptions. This has proven to be a great cross-promotional tool and was a big part of Jennifer Koch's (eBay User ID: thebridalcollection) decision to use Vendio as her auction management system. Another reason she enjoys their services is the automated feedback system. "When

TIP

Join the discussion at eBay Community to find out what auction tools other sellers are using. There are Community Help boards, Category Specific boards, General Discussion boards, as well as numerous Chat Rooms to find information, answers to questions, and new friends.

someone leaves me positive feedback, Vendio automatically posts feedback for them," she says. "I don't even have to think about it."

SellersSourcebook (www.sellersourcebook.com)

At the SellersSourcebook, sellers can find hundreds of professionally designed, specialty templates that require absolutely no HTML experience. Inge uses their templates in her jazzy-looking auctions, along with their easy-to-use image hosting services. In addition, they have coordinating About Me pages and automatic logo insertion, as well as a free auction tips newsletter, articles, and reviews about software, ebooks, and online tools.

Nucite (www.nucite.com)

For a low monthly subscription fee, you can have access to state-of-the-art auction templates and unlimited image hosting with the capability to watermark your pictures with your choice of text. Nucite's selection of free templates is limited, but the quality is excellent.

Auction Supplies (www.auctionsupplies.com)

Once you've gained some experience with HTML, you'll find the free auction templates on Auction Supplies interesting. In addition, they offer color charts and practice boards to see what your auction page will look like before you launch it, as well as image and HTML tutorials.

Photobucket (www.photobucket.com)

Photobucket is a favorite of Amy Caraluzzo (eBay User ID: princess*dreams*boutique) because it provides free limited image hosting for eBay users. However, if you need additional space you can upgrade to a premium account for a small fee. Other features include direct linking and online photo albums.

Security Central

Because online security is a big issue, part of your toolkit should include safety measures to protect you and your computer. Start by downloading the eBay Toolbar. This is a free, customizable toolbar that is downloaded to your Internet Explorer browser and provides direct links to preferred eBay pages. Whenever you are online it sends you alerts on auctions you are watching or bidding on, you can go to My eBay with one click, and use the handy search box for quick results. The toolbar's most popular feature is the Account Guard protection that lets you know when you are on a potentially fraudulent web site, while simultaneously protecting your account information.

Because spoof and phishing e-mails are so problematic, eBay recommends that you forward any suspicious e-mails to them at spoof@ebay.com for confirmation. Try to avoid clicking any links within the e-mail, but if you do, let Account Guard from the eBay Toolbar verify the site's authenticity. Also remember that eBay or PayPal will never ask you for personal account information such as your password,

BATTEN DOWN THE HATCHES

Take preventive steps to protect your computer from intruders. Michaels suggested imagining your eBay business is a brick-and-mortar store stocked with cash, employees, and merchandise. "Of course you're not just going to let somebody walk in and clean you out," she says. "It's going to be protected with an alarm, a padlock, and a safe. You have to secure your computer in the same way."

Recommended safety measures include:

- Installing a firewall in your computer
- Updating your virus software on a regular basis and scanning your computer frequently.
- Changing your password often; have a different one for each account, and *never* give them out to anyone.
- Online transactions should be made with a credit card (not a debit card) or a secure online payment service like PayPal.

credit card, bank account, or other personal information and you should not respond to those types of e-mails. Always check My eBay for copies of any messages that are sent from eBay.

Go to eBay's Security & Resolution Center (http://pages.ebay.com/securitycenter/) to learn more about safeguards around the eBay Marketplace, as well as general online safety. You will find information on deterring identity theft, avoiding fraud and online viruses, stopping spoof e-mails, and additional safety tips.

CHAPTER 10

Beating the Bushes

WITH MORE THAN 80 MILLION SEARCHES CONDUCTED ON eBay each day, sellers need to learn how to cull prospective buyers from that massive traffic flow and draw customers to their auctions and into their stores. This chapter describes different marketing tips, tricks, and techniques that will encourage browsers to stop, look, and buy, while identifying the competition and how to rise above it. Many people do not enjoy the prospect of marketing but it can be a lot of fun as you devise clever and innovative ideas to help line your silk pockets.

It's All About You!

Your About Me page is one of your best marketing tools—and it's free! This is the place where you and your business can shine by promoting existing auctions, your web site, or your eBay store. If you make custom items, this is a great place to advertise your craft and have customers contact you for special orders. Visitors can also find out more details on your policies, terms, and conditions that might be too lengthy to put in your auction descriptions. Because no one can physically walk into your eBay identity, your About Me page is the next best thing to a personal introduction.

In some ways, an About Me page is like a snazzy online brochure that can be used to win the trust and confidence of potential customers. "Bidders like to have a sense of who they are buying from," says Amy Caraluzzo (eBay User ID: princess*dreams*boutique). "I use mine as an opportunity to talk about the severe stroke my husband had two years ago, and how selling on eBay allows me to supplement his disability income."

You can design your own About Me page or use one of the templates that eBay provides for its members. How ever you set it up, make sure that you keep the information on it updated and consistent with concurrent auctions and activity in your store.

How Low Can You Go?

Ever wondered how some sellers can make a profit when they decide to sell certain items for pennies—like a brand-new

REVIEWS AND GUIDES

The Reviews and Guides section found on eBay's home page is a clever marketing tool that sellers can use to gain more exposure, while offering reviews, critiques, and advice to interested parties on a variety of topics. Under Reviews, members are encouraged to post their personal reviews about movies, books, music, games, electronic equipment, and other products. This helps shoppers know whether the item is worth investing in.

In the Guides section, members can write articles on any topic or category. For example, if you sell children's clothing you could offer advice on parenting issues or share kid-friendly recipes. Perhaps you have some eBay shopping tips that would benefit other users. In both the Reviews and Guides sections your User ID, Store, and About Me page will be prominently displayed and readers can vote on whether they found the information you posted helpful, while checking out your auctions or store.

designer handbag? This type of strategy is often used as a loss leader in an effort to draw visitors to their eBay store or web site. Retail stores have been doing this for years by selling certain items below cost in an attempt to attract customers. eBay store owners often promote auctions specifically designed to entice customers to take a peek with super-low starting bids. Once they have the customers' attention, they encourage them to step inside their stores and see all of their other wonderful items. Stephanie Inge (eBay User ID: stephintexas) says that sellers would never succeed without having traditional auctions running at all times. "Auctions are the big gorilla that draws in the foot traffic."

eBay Listing Upgrades

eBay has lots of way to help you make your listings more prominent. For an additional fee you can stand out in the crowd using the gallery feature, adding a border or bold text, or highlighting your listing with a different color, as well as use other clever techniques.

- *Gallery.* This is the most basic and popular of upgrades, which places a photo of your item next to the listing when it appears in search results. Lynda Ott-Albright (eBay User ID: shoppe*head2toe) says that she always uses gallery pictures in her listings and it really bugs her when other sellers do not. "When I'm browsing as a buyer, I look at the gallery pictures first to see what catches my eye," she says. "And if there is not a gallery picture, there better be a really good title to make me want to click that link."
- *Featured Plus!* This places your listing at the top of search results pages for the List View, and will be seen by people who browse by keyword or category. Jennifer

Koch (eBay User ID: thebridalcollection) says the Featured Plus! listings always help to keep her auctions at the front of the pack. "There are more than 6,000 wedding dresses listed on eBay at any given time, and it always shocks me that people can even find my stuff," she says. "I think its probably because I use the Featured Plus! tool." Occasionally she has launched an auction as a regular listing, but found those auctions did not receive nearly as much attention as the Featured Plus! listings.

- *Featured Gallery*. This options works just like Featured Plus! except your listing appears at the top of the page when browsers look at the Picture Gallery View, which is not the same as the predominantly used List View. An added bonus is that your picture will appear almost twice the size of the normal gallery listings.
- *Home Page Featured*. This is the greatest of listing upgrades because your listing will be featured on eBay's home page, as well as on its special Featured Items page. However, its value is questioned because of the small space featured items are given on the front page that sometimes go unnoticed. Although usually reserved for big-ticket items, the Home Page Featured is sometimes used for items as low as $10 in an effort to snag new visitors.
- *Item Subtitle*. This option allows you to put additional information about your item in a line that appears directly

under the title. Words in the subtitle will not appear in search results unless the browser is looking in both titles and descriptions. This can be a great marketing tool as it gives you the opportunity to expand on the features of the item being sold or used as a promotional tool for other merchandise you have. Koch uses the subtitle feature in every one of her listings to entice customers to look in her store for more wedding dress styles and sizes.

- *Highlight.* You can have your listing highlighted in purple to stand out in search results.
- *Bold.* Your auction title will be displayed in search results with a boldface font.
- *Border.* This option will wrap a colored band around your listing when it appears in search results.

TIP

Periodically eBay will offer steep discounts on various listing features to encourage you to try them. For example, sometimes eBay charges only a penny to add a subtitle, when it normally costs 50 cents, or you can get a border for a quarter over a two-day span. Watch for eBay listing specials by signing up for Announcements in the Community section of eBay.

- *List in Two Categories*. This feature doubles your auction's exposure by listing your item simultaneously in two different categories.
- *10-Day Duration*. Keeps your auction listed for an extra three days to give more browsers the opportunity to see it.
- *Scheduled Listings*. If time is an issue, you can arrange to have your listings launched at any date and time up to three weeks in advance.
- *Buy It Now*. This option gives buyers the opportunity to purchase your item immediately without waiting for the auction to end.
- *Gift Services*. Let buyers know that your item would make a great gift for which you can offer gift wrapping, gift cards, and shipping alternatives.
- *Listing Designer*. Provides a variety of templates and layouts to help you create professional auction listings. Using auction templates is also discussed in Chapter 9.

Smart Marketing Ideas

The following is a list of creative and successful marketing ideas.

- *Cross-Promote*. Whenever someone bids on or wins one of your auctions, four of your other listings are automatically shown in a display box for them to see. You have the ability to change and keep track of these cross-promotions from the "Items I'm Selling" view in My eBay.

- *Advertisements*. Few eBay sellers advertise their auctions offline, so taking this route may be intriguing. Start off small and choose local publications or newsletters where you can run a small classified or display ad. Briefly describe your niche and include the URL to locate the items on eBay. When you're feeling more adventurous, find a national publication such as a syndicated newspaper or popular magazine to advertise your eBay store or auctions.
- *eBay Keywords*. This powerful marketing tool is a service offered by adMarketplace that offers sellers the ability to place advertisements for their eBay stores or products above the usual eBay listings in the form of a text box or banner ad. Whenever specific keywords or phrases are typed in, these ads are prominently displayed at the top of the search results page. adMarketplace is a transparent, auction-based, pay-per-click system that allows sellers to decide how much they are willing to pay-per-click for each keyword. To learn more about eBay keywords and to sign up, visit www.ebaykeywords.com or www.admarketplace.net.
- *Signature Lines*. One of the best ways to promote your business in e-mails and on discussion boards is by providing direct links in your signature line. This simple marketing technique works as an unobtrusive promotional pitch—almost like a virtual business card. Keep it short with no more than two to three lines that include

a link to your eBay store, About Me page, or auction listings page.

- *Search Engine Optimization*. eBay is constantly updating its site and developing new tools to help sellers boost their search engine optimization results. This strategy increases your chances of having your eBay pages show up when people conduct keyword searches on search engines like Yahoo! or Google. Search engines use "web crawlers" to discover new information on the internet and because it takes a while for them to find new pages, search engine optimization will not be beneficial for short-term auction listings. However, eBay store listings, About Me pages, and submissions to Reviews and Guides that have all been optimized with relevant keywords and phrases can give you greater visibility to potential buyers.

TIP

If you have an eBay store, gift certificates can work as a customer reward and retention tool as well as a way to acquire new customers. For example, you may set up a rewards program and give a gift certificate of $5 for every $100 your customers spend in your eBay store during a specified time period. You can also encourage your existing customers to buy gift certificates as presents for family and friends.

- *Word-of-Mouth*. The most powerful form of marketing is word-of-mouth. Build a team of supporters by encouraging your family members, friends, associates, and non-eBay customers to check out your auctions and visit your eBay store so they can help spread the word about your eBay business. If you're offering quality merchandise, they'll be happy to help.
- *Shipping Inserts*. To generate repeat business and be memorable in your customers' minds, include a shipping insert in every package you send out. Such inserts can range from a thank-you card, flier, brochure, newsletter, discount coupon, or anything else that promotes your company. In addition to a handwritten note, Inge adds a surprise to every package she sends out. "I always try to give them more than what they are expecting." she says. "Then when they look at that pencil or eat that piece of candy, hopefully they will think about 'stephintexas' with a smile."

CHAPTER 11

How to Stuff **Your Stuff**

IN MOST EBAY TRANSACTIONS, THE BUYER PAYS FOR SHIPping, but that doesn't mean you don't have to worry about handling this part of the transaction effectively and efficiently. Because shipping can add substantially to the bottom-line cost of an item for bidders, many eBay sellers focus on products that are small, easy to pack, and don't cost a lot to ship.

Many eBay sellers say one of their biggest early mistakes was underestimating shipping charges. If you are setting a fixed shipping price in your auction (which is more and more difficult to do fairly and accurately because rates vary so much according to the package's destination), be sure you calculate it accurately. Amy Caraluzzo (eBay User ID: princess*dreams*boutique) says that a decent postage scale is essential so you can quote accurate shipping charges. It's highly impractical to stand on the bathroom scales and weigh yourself, then weigh again holding the item and subtract the difference. If you are shipping several items, you may have to weigh yourself several times a day and how fun is that? Plus, bathroom scales are notoriously inaccurate and will probably not reflect the actual weight. A good set of scales can be purchased at an office supply store, discount store, and on eBay. Some postage companies will even provide a free scale if you sign up for their service such as Stamps.com.

The eBay Shipping Calculator is a popular tool that can be automatically inserted into your auction listings. You can offer more than one shipping choice and have postage calculated for delivery to the buyer's zip code. The downside to this method is that sometimes buyers do not check the calculator before bidding and then are surprised at the close of the auction at how much shipping may cost. For this reason, many sellers prefer to insert a flat rate in the auction terms so there is no misunderstanding when it is time to finalize the transaction. Other sellers may ask interested buyers to contact them for shipping rates; however, this method is highly discouraged as you may lose a lot of customers who don't want to take the time to write and then wait for a response.

If you choose to set fixed shipping prices, when you're writing your auction description, weigh the item while you have it out and in your hands. Then add a pound or so (depending on how large and/or fragile it is) for packing materials. It's also reasonable to add a small charge to cover the cost of your packing materials. However, be fair with your shipping and handling charges. Certainly cover your costs, but resist the urge to make this a profit center. Experienced buyers will recognize that you're trying to make a profit on the shipping part of the sale, and they might not buy from you because of it.

Remember the adage "underpromise and overdeliver," and give yourself some wiggle room on your delivery commitments in case a situation comes up that is out of your control. For instance, deliveries may be delayed due to inclement weather. Sometimes packages are sent to the wrong address because the buyer neglected to update her eBay or PayPal account.

Without a doubt, shipping is a functional necessity, and it can be a disaster waiting to happen. But it can also be a marketing tool. Offer choices so your customers can select how fast they want to receive their merchandise and how much

TIP

Whenever possible, include the cost of shipping in your auction description so prospective buyers can take that into consideration when placing a bid.

they want to pay. Consider offering free shipping on big items, Buy It Now items or multiple purchases, or combine shipping on several small items.

Don't Just Toss It in a Box

Good packing is essential to protect your merchandise while it's in transit. Remember that your packages are going to be on a truck with other packages, they'll probably be loaded and unloaded several times, they'll likely experience bumps and vibrations, they may have other boxes stacked on top of them, and they may get dropped (or tossed around) repeatedly. All the "fragile" stickers in the world won't protect a carelessly packed shipment from damage.

Your best line of defense against freight damage is to pack your items to travel safely. Heed these tips:

- Use only sturdy cartons that can be completely sealed. Corrugated boxes are usually best.
- Pack firmly, but don't overload the box. Cartons should not rattle or bulge.
- Maintain a padded space between your item and the wall of the box to absorb shocks.
- Each item should be wrapped individually in tissue paper or cloth and separated from other items with sufficient cushioning to prevent damage from shock or vibration.
- Pack items in layers, placing the heaviest items on the bottom and the lightest on top.

- Do not pack hard or heavy items in the same box with fragile items.
- Seal each box completely with appropriate packaging tape. Don't use duct tape, electrical tape, cellophane tape, or masking tape on your packages. These tapes might be great for a variety of other functions, but they're not good for securing packages—they tend to peel off and/or deteriorate during transit. Do not use string; it can get caught in automated sorting equipment and damage both the equipment and your package. Paper overwrap is discouraged for the same reason.
- Label each carton with the name and address of both the shipper and the recipient. Number the boxes in the case of multicarton shipments (e.g., Box 1 of 2, Box 2 of 4, etc.).
- Include an inside label with complete shipper and recipient names and addresses in case anything happens to the outside label and it can't be read.

When using boxes, many shipping experts recommend using only new ones, but eBay sellers routinely reuse boxes with satisfactory results. If you are reusing a box, be sure it's in good condition, and remove any old labels and shipment markings. If you find that you use the same type of boxes again and again, buy them in bulk for added savings. eBay has many vendors that offer packing and shipping supplies at reduced costs.

In addition to boxes, eBay clothing sellers use a variety of mailers to ship their items, including Tyvek, poly, paper, and

TIP

The buyer will be excited about receiving his purchase, so package your items as if you were presenting a gift. For example, you wouldn't give Aunt Bessie a lace nightie crammed in an envelope would you? Wrap it carefully in tissue paper and secure it with a ribbon. It will only take a couple of extra minutes to make an impact and brighten someone's day.

bubble mailers. If the mailer you're using isn't waterproof, place the garments in a plastic bag for added protection. Many buyers live in residences where the carrier will have to leave the package exposed to the elements and a torrential rain storm could ruin the beautiful silk scarf your buyer ordered.

Choosing a Carrier

There is a wide range of differences in the pricing and service levels of various package and freight carriers, and it's a good idea to become familiar with them before making a decision on which carrier to use. Customers will view your choice of carrier and the service it provides as an extension of your operation, so it's important to use one that delivers a high level of customer service and reliability. Don't make your decision based on cost alone; as important as price is, the lowest price is not always the best value. Convenience is another factor as some carriers will offer pick-up services from your front door, a service that Caraluzzo takes advantage of frequently from the USPS.

It's important to understand the difference between a package carrier and a common carrier. Common carriers are truck lines that handle large, heavy shipments that are too big for the package carriers. Package carriers (such as UPS, FedEx, DHL, and the USPS) handle smaller shipments with per-package weight limits typically ranging from 70 to 150 pounds. Many offer a choice of ground or air service. Caraluzzo generally likes to mail her items via USPS Priority Mail; however, she says, "As a cost reduction I will use Parcel Post or First Class if the item is light enough." Lynda Ott-Albright (eBay User ID: shoppe*head2toe) also prefers the USPS for most of her items, although she uses FedEx when she has larger boxes to ship. On the other hand, Jennifer Koch (eBay User ID: thebridalcollection) always uses UPS for shipping because she likes their tracking feature and free insurance coverage up to $100.

When choosing a carrier, points to consider include:

- What are the size and weight limitations, and how does that compare with what you are shipping?
- What levels of service are available?
- Does the carrier offer online package tracking? How easy or difficult is it to use?
- Will the carrier make multiple delivery attempts without charging an extra fee?

- Does the carrier offer e-mail notification to let your customer know the package is on the way?
- Does the carrier deliver on Saturdays and, if so, is there an extra charge?
- How late will the carrier make pickups at your facility, and how does this blend with your work schedule?
- Does the carrier have a facility where your customers can pick up their packages? (This is known as "hold for pickup.")
- Does the carrier offer return services to help you retrieve packages if necessary?
- Will the carrier provide delivery confirmation and, if so, is there an extra charge?
- Is the carrier financially stable?

Carrier selection is important not only for what you are shipping out but also for what you receive. If you are paying the freight on your incoming materials, you have the right to name the carrier. Beyond that, as a matter of good customer service, your suppliers should be willing to honor your carrier choice.

International Shipping Is a Plus

Many eBay sellers don't like to ship overseas because they don't understand the process or find it to be too much work. But if you take the time to learn how to do it—and for most countries, it's not complicated—you can increase your profits significantly. Willingness to ship internationally can give you an edge over sellers who won't do it.

MAKE LABELING A SNAP

Thanks to new and constantly improving online shipping tools, most sellers can print labels from their computers rather than creating them by hand. PayPal and eBay have a combined feature at the close of the auction where you can go to the auction page or My eBay and simply click a link to generate a label. This will print out a shipping label with the buyer's name and address and pre-calculated postage on it without having to type anything other than your password. There is a nominal processing fee that will be deducted from your PayPal account along with the postage, but the time savings may be worth it. There are also many other auction management tools that will calculate postage and print out labels with or without postage.

Stamps.com (www.stamps.com) and Endicia Online Postage (www.endicia.com) are two of several timesaving postage systems for sellers that ship a high volume of items. You can print out labels with any type of official USPS postage (i.e., Express, Media, First Class) to be delivered anywhere in the world. They offer competitive monthly subscription fees and free trial periods.

USPS (www.usps.gov) has a Click-N-Ship feature that will print labels with postage and insurance for Priority, Express, or Global (international) Mail by using your credit card. You can also download a free software program called Shipping Assistant that can be used to calculate domestic and international rates using any of the postal services, including First Class, Media Mail, and Parcel Post, as well as Priority and Express Mail.

Most major couriers, such as UPS (www.ups.com) and FedEx (www.fedex.com), have similar online features, plus you can often schedule pick-ups from your home or office online without having to make a phone call.

Koch says that quite a few of her wedding dresses go overseas. "While the bulk of my business is within the United States, I send a lot of dresses to Australia, Japan, Canada, and some of the European countries."

The package and freight companies that deliver overseas (USPS, UPS, FedEx, DHL, etc.) have plenty of information to help you understand the procedures and paperwork necessary to ship to various international destinations. Contact the individual companies, or visit their web sites for details.

Insurance Benefits

Insurance protects you and your customers by paying to replace or repair items that are damaged in transit. For high-end or very fragile merchandise, insist that your buyers pay for insurance for the full value of the goods. For low-end or very sturdy merchandise, you may allow buyers to make the choice of whether to buy insurance. But stress that if they reject insurance, your responsibility ends with shipping. Be sure you can prove that you shipped the merchandise, either by using a carrier (such as UPS or FedEx) that will provide you with a shipper's receipt, or by using the delivery confirmation service offered by the USPS.

Some carriers automatically provide coverage for loss or damage up to $100 per shipment at no extra charge; others charge for the first dollar of insurance coverage. Don't bother to buy insurance for more than you can prove the item is worth; the carrier will only reimburse you for the actual value, not for the amount of insurance you purchased. Documents that are generally accepted as proof of value include a current bill of sale, an invoice, or a statement from a certified appraiser.

Even when you purchase insurance, it's important that your items be properly packed for transit. If damage occurs and the carrier determines that the shipment was not appropriately packed, your claim (or the buyer's claim, in most cases) will likely be denied.

Some sellers prefer to "self-insure" packages, which is fine if you are guaranteeing delivery and willing to pay for damages out of your own pocket. However, be aware that many states have regulations about offering insurance and require an individual to be licensed or bonded. This means you cannot charge a separate insurance fee if you are self-insuring.

TIP

Clearly define your shipping policy within your auction description and on your About Me page by stating the cost of shipping, who will pay (usually the buyer), what service you will use, and what days you traditionally ship on.

Delivery Confirmation

You can significantly decrease the risk of buyers claiming they never received a package by using the USPS delivery confirmation. This inexpensive service can give you peace of mind while tracking the shipment of packages across the country. Rates are typically lower—sometimes free—for sellers who purchase postage electronically. However, note that while delivery confirmation is used to verify delivery of auction goods, it does not insure packages against damages.

CHAPTER 12

Crunching **the Numbers**

THE BEST INDICATOR OF HOW SERIOUS YOU ARE ABOUT your eBay business is how you handle the money. And if you're serious about your business, you need to be serious about the money. Basically there are two sides to the issue of money: how much you need to start and operate, and how much you can expect to take in.

Start-Up Funds

It takes very little cash to start selling things on eBay, especially if you begin by selling things you already own or are adding another sales venue to an existing business. Amy Caraluzzo (eBay User ID:

princess*dreams*boutique) agrees, as she needed very little in the way of start-up funds. "I had bins and bins of children's clothing that had been outgrown; plus I already had a computer and a digital camera," she says. "The only other thing I really needed was a printer which I found through a local Freecycle group."

You may decide you need additional funds to invest in inventory, upgraded facilities, new services, and more sophisticated equipment. Start-up money needs to cover your inventory, equipment, supplies, and working capital. Inventory includes the merchandise you're going to sell. Equipment includes your computer, printer, digital camera, scanner, telephone, scales, and anything else you need to operate. Supplies include paper, labels, boxes, packing material, tape, and even small things like sticky notes and staples. Most of these items are relatively inexpensive, but they can add up.

So, where is the money? Take a look at the following sections for some ideas.

Personal Resources

When thinking of creative ways to come up with start-up funds, consider your own resources. People generally have more in the way of assets than they realize. Make a list of what you have, including savings and retirement accounts, equity in real estate, vehicles, collections, and other investments. Though you may not want to sell your car or siphon funds from your retirement account to finance your eBay business, you may be willing to sell the Barbie doll collection that you haven't looked at in years. If you don't want to sell your assets for cash, think about using them as collateral for a loan. Or auction things you already own to raise cash to invest in inventory and equipment.

Credit Cards

Many successful businesses, both on and off eBay, have been jump-started with plastic. Just be smart about it because sky-high interest rates could bury you for years. If you do use a credit card to help fund your eBay business, only charge items that will contribute to revenue generation. For example, a digital camera can speed up the time it takes to launch an auction and eliminate film processing expenses, which makes it an acceptable item to charge.

Friends and Family

A lot of start-ups have been funded with seed money from friends and relatives who recognized the potential value of the venture and wanted to help their loved ones succeed. However, be cautious with these arrangements; no matter how close you are, present yourself professionally, put everything in writing, and be sure the individuals you approach can afford to take the risk of investing in your business. Never accept money for a business venture from anyone who can't afford to lose that money.

Partners

Most operations that sell on eBay are owned by just one person or perhaps a married couple, but there are plenty of successful partnerships. When considering partners as a funding source, you may look for someone who has financial resources and also wants to work side by side with you in the business. Or you may find someone who has money to invest but no interest in doing the actual work. As with your friends and family, be sure to create a written partnership agreement that clearly defines your respective responsibilities and obligations.

Government Programs

Take advantage of the abundance of local, state, and federal programs designed to support small business. First check with the U.S. Small Business Administration (www.sba.gov), then look into various other programs that may offer funding or support. Women, minorities, and veterans should check out niche financing possibilities designed to help these groups get into business. Your local economic development agency may have local and state grants or low-interest loans available.

How Will You Get Paid?

Decide in advance what payment methods you will accept because it's something many bidders consider before placing a bid. Your payment terms should be clearly stated in your auction listings and on your About Me page. Electronic payments (credit cards, debit cards, and e-checks) are the most popular methods of paying for auction goods, but don't make your decision based solely on what's best and easiest for you. Develop a plan for using payment options that will make you an attractive seller to potential customers and contribute to your success.

- *PayPal*. eBay's subsidiary PayPal (www.paypal.com) is the site's preferred payment method and the most popular online payment service. PayPal is free to buyers and allows them to pay with their credit cards, debit cards, bank accounts, or PayPal balance without revealing their private financial information to the seller.
- *Personal Checks*. Some sellers are reluctant to accept personal checks because of the risk that the check might bounce. The real reason to avoid personal checks is that they're a nuisance to deal with because of the additional paperwork and time involved with handling them. Although some sellers refuse to accept personal checks,

TIP

If accepting personal checks is a concern, you can always encourage buyers to have an electronic check issued through PayPal, which only takes three to four days to process. The waiting period will be much shorter for both of you.

think carefully before establishing this policy as it may turn away prospective bidders.

- *Money Orders and Cashier's Checks.* There is little risk in accepting money orders, cashier's checks, and other forms of certified funds. In the unlikely event that the check is lost in the mail, the buyer can initiate a trace and replacement. The biggest drawback to this payment type is the same as with personal checks: it adds time to the transaction and is more paperwork for you.
- *Escrow Service.* An escrow service is usually reserved for high-priced items by using a third party to collect the payment from the buyer and hold the funds until the merchandise has been delivered and the buyer is satisfied. The process protects both the seller, who doesn't ship until the funds have been received by the escrow service, and the buyer, because the escrow service holds the funds until she authorizes the payment to be made.
- *Credit Card Merchant Accounts.* Some eBay sellers, particularly those who sell in high volume and/or have other sales venues, choose to accept credit and debit cards by opening merchant accounts. This is a convenience for buyers who would like to pay by credit or debit card, but do not have or want a PayPal account.

Financial Management

If you want to build a serious and profitable eBay business, a sound financial plan is essential. It begins with knowing what you need, what you have, what's coming in, and what's going out. To know that you need to keep thorough and complete financial records.

Keeping good records helps generate the financial statements that tell you exactly where you stand and what you need to do next. The key financial statements you need to understand and use regularly are:

- *Profit and loss statement (also called the P&L or the income statement)*. This statement illustrates how much your company is making or losing over a designated period—monthly, quarterly, or annually—by subtracting expenses from your revenue to arrive at a net result, which is either a profit or a loss.
- *Balance sheet.* A balance sheet is a table showing your assets, liabilities, and capital at a specific point. A balance sheet is typically generated monthly, quarterly, or annually when the books are closed.
- *Cash flow statement.* This summarizes the operating, investing, and financing activities of your business as they relate to the inflow and outflow of cash. As with the profit and loss statement, a cash flow statement is prepared to reflect a specific accounting period, such as monthly, quarterly, or annually.

Successful eBay sellers review these reports regularly, at least monthly, so they always know where they stand and can quickly move to correct minor difficulties before they become major financial problems.

TIP

Don't mix business with personal—accounts that is. Keep separate business checking accounts and credit cards to help maintain accurate records.

Taxing Matters

Businesses are required to pay a wide range of taxes, and there are no exceptions for companies that sell on eBay. Keep accurate records so you can offset your local, state, and federal income taxes with your operating expenses. Take the time to review all your tax liabilities with your accountant.

Income Tax

E-commerce venues such as eBay and other auction sites are being carefully scrutinized by the Internal Revenue Service (IRS) these days. Also, many financial institutions report to the IRS how much nonemployment money individuals deposit in their accounts. You must report all your income from your eBay sales, no matter how insignificant. Failing to do so is a crime. If a government bean counter starts pouring over your books, a defense of "I didn't think you would catch me" isn't going to be much value if you are caught not reporting income.

Cathi Aiello of Allegro Accounting, Inc. says that 40 percent of her business consists of working with eBay sellers.

"What many sellers don't realize when they're out shopping for new inventory at garage sales and clothing outlets is that the minute they buy something to resell, they have just gone into business for themselves and now have tax issues." Aiello did stress that the same rules do not apply to personal items that you are selling out of your home. Income from those sales is not taxable and the expenses are not deductible. "But if the money hitting your bank account is questioned in an audit, you will need to prove the money came from the sale of personal items. So keep good records," she advises.

Of course, in addition to reporting all your income, you should take every single deduction to which you are legally entitled. Homebased businesses may qualify for the home office deduction, which allows you to deduct a portion of your rent, mortgage interest, household utilities and services, real estate taxes, homeowner's insurance, repairs, security systems, and depreciation. If you're driving back and forth to the post office or another shipping location, you can either deduct mileage or depreciate your car and write off the actual expenses. Also keep track of your listing fees, final value fees, PayPal fees, and other selling-related fees. Finally, consult with a qualified tax advisor to determine what deductions you may take.

Sales Tax

A potentially sticky area for online auction sellers is sales tax. Many large retailers with online operations have begun

WHAT'S IN THE FORECAST?

You don't need a crystal ball to predict future revenue, but you do need a formula to foresee how much you can expect to make in the weeks, months, and years ahead, as these numbers will become your sales goals. The challenge for new eBay sellers—as it is for any new business owner—is figuring out what your sales are likely to be when you don't have a history to use as a basis.

Study the pricing strategies discussed in Chapter 5. Next, consider how many auctions you'll be able to launch per week or month, how many items you can expect to stock in your eBay store, what your average sale will be, and what percentage of those auctions and store listings are likely to result in completed sales. Your initial revenue forecasts will likely need revising as you begin operations and see actual results.

Keep track of your average selling price (ASP). If, for example, most of your auctions close with a final value price of less than $10, you have to sell and ship a lot of items to make a decent living. Track your ASP and look for ways to increase it. Can you add new accessories? Sell in larger quantities? For most eBay sellers who are getting a decent margin on their products, an ASP of $30 to $50 will give you a worthwhile return.

collecting sales tax on their internet sales, and legislation affecting how internet sales are taxed is pending at state and federal levels. As a business owner, you are responsible for knowing the law and doing the right thing.

To charge and collect sales tax, you'll need a sales tax ID number (sometimes referred to as a reseller's permit) which is usually as simple as filling out a form. Check with your state's department of revenue for information on how to get a tax ID number.

CHAPTER 13

Help Wanted

PLENTY OF EBAY SELLERS MAKE COMFORTABLE INCOMES AS solo operators, handling everything themselves. They're happy keeping their businesses as one-person operations and have no desire to do anything different. While there's nothing wrong with this strategy, if your goal is growth, you will reach a point where you must hire people. And even if your goal isn't growth, there may be times when you need help, so it's important to understand the basics of finding, hiring, and managing personnel.

You may find it difficult to delegate tasks to someone else, especially if you've never supervised or managed people before. There's little anyone can tell you to make this leap easier; you just have to do it—and believe that it will be worth the effort. As your business grows, don't make the mistake of trying to do too much yourself and not hiring customer service staffers soon enough.

With this in mind, let's consider the process of adding staff to your operation. The first step is to decide exactly what you want someone to do and write a job description. The job description you write doesn't have to be as formal as one you might expect from a large corporation, but it needs to clearly outline the person's duties and responsibilities. It should also list any special skills or other required credentials, such as a valid driver's license and clean driving record for someone who is going to take packages to the post office and run other errands for you, or computer skills for administrative help. Next, you need to establish a pay scale. This will depend on what you are hiring people to do, the skills needed, and the pay scales in your area.

You should also have a job application form. You can get a basic form at most office supply stores or you can create your own. Have your attorney review the form you will be using for compliance with the most current employment laws. Every prospective employee should fill out an application—even if it's someone you already know, and even if she has submitted a detailed resume. A resume is not a signed, sworn statement acknowledging that you can fire her if she lies; the application is. The application will also help you verify resumes; compare the two and make sure the information is consistent. Now you're ready to start looking for candidates.

Where Are Your Future Employees?

Picture the ideal candidate in your mind. Is this person a stay-at-home mom who could use a part-time job a few days a week, or is it a super-efficient administrative assistant who can whip your office into shape?

Network with personal and professional associates to identify prospective employees—you never know who might know the perfect person for your company. Check with nearby colleges and perhaps even high schools for part-time help.

Another option is to use a temporary help or employment agency. Many small businesses shy away from agencies because they feel like they can't afford the fee—but if the agency handles the advertising, initial screening, and background checks,

TIP

Decide what type of manager you are before hiring someone. If you're a hands-on kind of person, an independent thinker may not appreciate your style. But if you need an employee to take the proverbial bull by the horns, you may be annoyed with someone who requires a lot of direction and feedback.

the fee may be well worth paying. Use caution if you decide to hire friends and relatives—many personal relationships have not been strong enough to survive an employee-employer situation.

Evaluating Applicants

What kinds of people make good employees for a company that sells on eBay? It depends on what you want them to do. If you're hiring someone as a driver, that person should have a good driving record and know the city. If you're hiring someone to help with administrative tasks, he needs to have computer knowledge and be able to learn your operating system. If you're hiring someone to handle customer service, he needs to know your products and policies, care about people, and be able to react quickly and calmly to surprises. What is really important is that the people you hire are committed to giving you their best effort during the time they're working so that your customers receive the best service.

It's a good idea to prepare your interview questions in advance. Develop open-ended questions that encourage the candidate to talk. In addition to knowing what they've done, you want to find out how they did it. Ask each candidate the same set of questions, and make notes as they respond so you can make an accurate assessment and comparison later.

When the interview is over, let the candidate know what to expect. Is it going to take you several weeks to interview other candidates, check references and make a decision? Will you want the top candidates to return for a second interview? Will you call the candidates, or should they call you? This is not only a good business practice, it's also simple common courtesy.

Always check the former employers and personal references of your candidates. Though many companies are very restrictive as to what information they'll verify, you may be surprised at what you can find out. You should at least confirm that the applicant told the truth about dates and positions held. Personal references are likely to give you some additional insight into the general character and personality of the candidate. This will help you decide if she will be a match for your culture and fit into your operation.

Be sure to document every step of the interview and reference-checking process. Even very small companies are finding themselves the targets of employment discrimination suits; good records are your best defense if it happens to you.

Once They're On Board

The hiring process is only the beginning of the challenge of having employees. The next thing you need to do is train them. Don't just throw someone into the job; that's not fair to the employee, and it's certainly not good for your business. You can't afford not to take the time to adequately train an employee. Do you really want him interacting with your customers when you haven't told him how you want things done? Be clear and let employees know when they have done something well and, tactfully and constructively, let them know when they are doing less than an adequate job.

Employee Benefits

The wages you pay may be only part of your employees' total compensation. While many very small companies do not offer a formal benefits program, more and more business owners have recognized that benefits—particularly in the area of health insurance—are extremely important when it comes to attracting and retaining quality employees. Regardless of the overall employment situation, competition for good people is stiff almost everywhere.

Typical benefit packages include group insurance (your employees may pay all or a portion of their premiums), paid holidays, and vacations. You can build employee loyalty by seeking additional benefits that may be somewhat unusual—and they don't have to cost much. For example, Karyn Michaels (eBay User ID: whattachloegirl) lets her five part-time employees buy whatever they want from her inventory at cost, so they get some really great bargains and she has happy employees.

Short-Term Solutions

If your staffing needs fluctuate, consider using a temporary labor service as a source for workers when your regular full-time staff is not enough. You may also find that certain tasks can be handled by an independent contractor or consultant.

WORKERS' COMPENSATION INSURANCE

In most states, if you have three or more employees, you are required by law to carry workers' compensation insurance. This coverage pays medical expenses and replaces a portion of the employee's wages if he or she is injured on the job. Even if you have only one or two employees, you may want to consider obtaining this coverage to protect both them and you in the event of an accident.

Details and requirements vary by state; contact your state's insurance office or your own insurance agent for information so you can be sure you're in compliance.

Consider outsourcing work in the areas of accounting and record-keeping, special marketing projects, and so on. If you have tasks you need help with but that don't fit the parameters of a regular part- or full-time position, look for nontraditional ways to get them done.

CHAPTER 14

Snags, Snarls, and Snickers

HOPEFULLY BY THIS POINT YOU HAVE A GOOD, SOLID IDEA of what to do—or not to do—as an eBay seller. In this concluding chapter we will wrap things up by offering final words of wisdom, tales from the trenches, and humorous anecdotes to help inspire and motivate you as you set forth on this new venture. Fortified with sage advice and clever ideas found in this book, there is no time like the present to begin selling clothing, shoes, and accessories through the world's largest online emporium—eBay!

Expanding Your Horizons

When Lynda Ott-Albright (eBay User ID: shoppe*head2toe) was looking for specific European designer clothing, she decided to look on eBay Netherlands (www.ebay.nl) and eBay Germany (www.ebay.de). The fact that both of these sites were in foreign languages did not deter Ott-Albright from her mission. She was able to find an online translation program that translated auction descriptions from German or Dutch to English. If she had a question for the seller, she would use the translation program to write it in his native language. "I have found some wonderful sellers overseas, including a lady making custom designs out of Oilily material," she says. "I definitely want to continue doing business with her."

Let's Go Dancing!

Anyone who clicks into one of Stephanie Inge's (eBay User ID: stephintexas) auctions will find themselves serenaded by Lee Ann Womack or tapping toes along with Deryl Dodd or Gretchen Wilson. "Over the last few months I have tried to make my auctions a multimedia experience," she says. "I incorporated the music to get buyers in the mood to go country and western dancing, or just to have fun looking at all of the boots." Her strategy has worked well because she gets tons of visitors who not only want to look at her auctions, but also listen to the catchy tunes coming across the cyber waves.

Online Safety

Most eBay clothing sellers agree that displaying clothing and accessories to their best advantage works best with a live model to give sales a boost. However, what many sellers cannot agree on is whether or not it's safe or appropriate to use children as live models in their auctions, so we talked to Sargent Kevin Stenger, Supervisor of the Computer Crimes Squad for the Orange County, Florida Sheriff's Office. He says there has never been a problem reported with anyone abusing a child's photograph on eBay. "Although it is possible that someone could download a kid's picture and paste them over nudes, they hardly ever do that because unfortunately, they can easily get their hands on the real stuff." However, Sgt. Stenger says it is a concern when sellers identify their children in the auction or on About Me pages, which they should never do. With over 80 million searches conducted on eBay each day, please be cautious about what type of personal information you post.

Using Auction Templates

Amy Caraluzzo (eBay User ID: princess*dreams*boutique) feels that if you are serious about your eBay business, your auctions have to look professional. Auction templates can be found all over the internet—some are free, and others have a fee. Caraluzzo says that she has a large collection of templates that she has collected over time and many of them came from participating on Yahoo! Groups lists specifically for auction templates. "Membership is free and so are the templates, so why pay money for them elsewhere? That will just bring your profits down." she says.

The Doctor Is In

Dr. eBay (a/k/a/ Stephanie Inge) has the right prescription for your eBay success. Inge is one of many eBay Certified Education Specialists that teach eBay sellers around the country. She offers free advice, hands-on training, business consulting, consignment selling, and many valuable resources to help your business grow to its full potential. "The smartest thing I ever did was take my eBay instruction classes to the college level," she says. "It has brought a whole new dimension to my business, not to mention a constant stream of revenue." If you would like to find a Certified Education Specialist in your area, go to the Education Program Specialist Directory at: www.poweru.net/ebay/student/searchIndex.asp

Back to School

If attending local eBay classes is not a viable option, do the next best thing and go the distance. Distance learning that is. The eBay University offers online courses for buyers and sellers taught by experts just like Dr. eBay. Online workshops are also available on a variety of topics such as branding and merchandising, packing and shipping basics, tax structures, accounting, feedback, and more. Participating in a live chat workshop is a great learning experience because it gives members the opportunity to ask questions and receive fast answers. But do not despair if you are unable to attend the workshop of your choice, because transcripts from the workshop will be made available afterwards. For more information, look for workshops under the Community link.

Be a Part of the Community

Participating on eBay discussion forums is another great way to learn new tips, tricks, and strategies, while staying on top of auction market news, events, and information. In addition to the discussion boards in the Community section of eBay, other popular auction-related discussion groups can be found on eBay, Yahoo!, Topica, AOL, and MSN. Karen Michaels (eBay User ID: whattachloegirl) is a regular contributor to online discussion forums, as are Ott-Albright, Inge, and Caraluzzo. "I just feel that everybody you meet can teach you something." Michaels says. "Each seller runs her business in a different way and you can find out so much information just by listening to them and asking questions."

Future Goals: Becoming a PowerSeller

PowerSellers are eBay's most successful sellers in terms of product sales and customer satisfaction. To achieve this esteemed designation, a seller has to meet a monthly sales quota and maintain a positive feedback rating of 98 percent or higher. There are five PowerSeller levels: Bronze, Silver, Gold, Platinum, and Titanium, and each is based on gross monthly sales.

Though there is no charge to become a Power Seller, it is not an automatic process. eBay monitors sales activity and each month sends out invitations to qualified sellers. Sellers who accept the invitation appreciate the status that comes with the title. It tells buyers that the seller is serious about his business and committed to upholding eBay's high standards.

In addition to the PowerSeller symbol proudly displayed by your user ID, perks include enhanced technical and customer support, as well as publications, promotional offers, eBay promotional merchandise, advanced selling education, opportunities to participate in research, and more.

Accepting the PowerSeller designation means committing to maintaining a specific monthly sales level and agreeing to the PowerSeller Rules, such as having a no-questions-asked return policy. Whether you choose to accept the PowerSeller invitation is a decision you have to make based on your particular business and operating style. But qualifying for the designation is a worthwhile goal for your eBay operation.

APPENDIX

Resource Guide

eBay Sites of Interest

eBay Business Marketplace
www.ebaybusiness.com
For the small business owner.

eBay Help
http://pages.ebay.com/help/index.html
Find the answers to all of your eBay questions here.

eBay Keywords
www.ebaykeywords.com or www.admarketplace.net
Find out how to increase your sales using keywords.

eBay's Used Clothing Policy
http://pages.ebay.com/help/policies/used-clothing.html

Education Program Specialist Directory
www.poweru.net/ebay/student/searchIndex.asp
To locate a Certified Education Specialist in your area.

International Trading Center
http://pages.ebay.com/internationaltrading
Tips and tools for eBayers who want to buy and sell outside of the United States.

Security & Resolution Center
http://pages.ebay.com/securitycenter
This is the place to go for payment, transaction, or payment issues.

Seller Central
http://pages.ebay.com/sellercentral
The best place to go for the latest tips, tools, information, and resources for selling on eBay, including What's Hot and the eBay Pulse.

Internet Resources

Disabled Online Users Association (DOUA)
www.doua.org
A network of individuals who are learning and teaching how to earn a living by selling on the internet.

Federal Trade Commission
www.ftc.gov

Flea Market Guide
http://fleamarketguide.com
Comprehensive listing of U.S. flea markets.

Internet Auction List
www.internetauctionlist.com

National Association of Wholesaler-Distributors
www.naw.org

Online Traders Web Alliance (OTWA)
www.otwa.com
An online auction association dedicated to the independent online auction seller and merchant.

Tax Saving Educational Tools
http://taxloopholes.com

U.S. Department of State
www.state.gov
Good site to visit when shopping for overseas suppliers and/or to find out information on different countries. Also has links to web sites of U.S. embassies and consulates around the world.

U.S. Small Business Administration
www.sba.gov
Information and support for small businesses.

Worldwide Brands
www.worldwidebrands.com
Drop-shipping, wholesale, and home business information.

Online Payment Resources

Escrow.com
www.escrow.com
Escrow service used by eBay; accepts payments by credit cards, PayPal, checks, wire transfers, money orders, and cashier's checks.

PayPal
www.paypal.com
Subsidiary of eBay. Free for buyers; sellers pay a percentage fee to use its services.

Auction Management Tools and Templates

Andale
www.andale.com
Has many auction tools including research, store, and management; also includes free counters.

AuctionPix
www.auctionpix.com
Offers two options for hosting images: pay per image or for designated space.

Auction Supplies
www.auctionsupplies.com

Free auction templates, color chart, and practice boards.

MarketWorks
www.marketworks.com
Comprehensive list of auction tools and services.

Nucite
www.nucite.com
State-of-the-art auction templates and unlimited image hosting.

Photobucket
www.photobucket.com
Free photo hosting.

SellersSourcebook
www.sellersourcebook.com
Has hundreds of professionally designed, specialty themed templates.

SpareDollar
www.sparedollar.com
Auction management services.

ViewTracker™
www.sellathon.com
Tracking software that gives you tons of stats on visitors to your auctions.

Vendio
www.vendio.com
Provides image hosting and many other auction tools, including research, inventory control, auction management and more.

Miscellaneous Tools

Free Misspelled Words Toolbar
www.misspellsearch.com

Froogle
www.froogle.com
A shopping tool that can help you find out what specific items are selling for on the internet.

JPEG Magic
www.jpegmagic.com
Image optimizer and compressor tool with an easy interface for rotating, lightening, and darkening photos.

Nameboy.com
www.nameboy.com
Nickname generator

Overture's free keyword suggestion tool
http://inventory.overture.com/d/searchinventory/suggestion

Wordtracker
www.wordtracker.com
Online ticker featuring the top 50 items searched for in the past 24 hours. Also has a free keyword weekly report with 500 of the most frequently searched keywords.

Online Shipping and Postage Resources

DHL
www.dhl-usa.com

Endicia Online Postage
www.endicia.com

FedEx
www.fedex.com

Smart Shipping
www.smartshipping.com
A variety of shipping resources, including carriers, supplies, and services.

Stamps.com
www.stamps.com

UPS
www.ups.com

USPS
www.usps.gov

Successful eBay Sellers

Amy Caraluzzo
Atco, New Jersey
eBay User ID: Princess*Dreams*Boutique

Stephanie Inge
Rowlett, Texas
Store: http://stores.ebay.com/TEXAS-STATE-OF-MIND
Web site: www.dr-ebay.com/
eBay User ID: (stephintexas)

Jennifer Koch
Portage, Michigan
Store: http://stores.ebay.com/The-Bridal-Collection
eBay User ID: thebridalcollection

Karyn Michaels
Bucks County, Pennsylvania
Store: http://stores.ebay.com/DesignRKidz
eBay User ID: WhattaChloeGirl

Lynda Ott-Albright
Pasadena, California
Store: http://stores.ebay.com/Head-2-Toe-Shoppe
eBay User ID: shoppe*head2toe

Consultants and Other Experts

Cathi Aiello
Allegro Accounting, Inc.
Sherwood, Oregon
www.allegroaccounting.com

Sargent Kevin Stenger
Supervisor of the Computer Crimes Squad
Orange County Sheriff's Office
Orlando, Florida

Publications

Make BIG Profits on eBay: Start Your Own Million $ Business
Jacquelyn Lynn and Charlene Davis (Entrepreneur Press, 2005)

202 Things You Can Buy and Sell for Big Profits
James Stephenson (Entrepreneur Press, 2004)

The Official eBay Bible
Jim "Griff" Griffith (Gotham, 2003)

Starting Your Online Auction Business
Denis L. Prince (Prima Tech, 2000)

Glossary

About Me. An eBay page that tells other users about you, your merchandise, and your selling terms and conditions.

Advanced Search. A detailed search that allows you to find specific eBay users, look for items using different keyword strategies, and search completed listings.

Auction Management Software. Software that allows sellers to monitor auctions and perform listing activities in one place.

Best Offer. Allows buyers to suggest a price they are willing to pay for an item; this is a free feature but must be used in conjunction with Buy It Now.

Bid. A buyer enters the maximum amount he or she is willing to pay for an item, which is increased incrementally; considered binding unless retracted or cancelled.

Bid Cancellation. The cancellation of a bid by a buyer or seller.

Bid Increment. The amount by which a bid is increased each time the current bid is outdone.

Bid Retraction. Withdrawing a bid; bid retractions are rarely allowed on eBay.

Bid Shielding. Using secondary user IDs or other eBay members to temporarily raise the level of bidding to extremely high levels in order to protect the low bid level of another bidder; when bid shielding, the high bidder retracts the bid before the auction closes.

Blocked Bidder List. A list of eBay users who are blocked from bidding on another user's auctions.

Buy It Now (BIN). A feature that allows buyers to purchase an item for a fixed price, bypassing the bidding process; can be used in auction-style or fixed-price listings.

Community. A term used to identify eBay members, including buyers and sellers, who can also chat on discussion forums, boards, and groups.

Completed Search. A search of eBay auctions that have ended.

Dimensional Weight. A standard formula used in the freight industry that considers a package's density when determining charges; charges are based on the actual weight or the dimensional weight, whichever is greater.

Discount. The amount by which a price is reduced to create an incentive for various consumer behaviors, such as to increase sales or encourage early payment.

Discussion Board. An area within the eBay Community where members can discuss eBay-related topics.

Drop-Ship. When merchandise is shipped to your customer from a location other than your own as though it was being shipped by you.

Dutch Auction. When the seller has two or more identical items offered in the same auction; also known as a *Multiple Item Auction.*

eBay Shipping Calculator. A tool sellers can insert in auction descriptions that allows buyers to determine how much shipping will cost to their ZIP codes.

eBay Stores. A venue for sellers to promote inventory through fixed-price listings.

eBay Toolbar. A collection of tools primary used by bidders that sits on your desktop as a single block of buttons.

Featured Listing: A marketing service provided by eBay that gives auctions extra exposure in the "Featured" sections at the top of listings pages

Feedback. Comments made by one user about another regarding the trading experience between the two.

Final Value Fee. The percentage of the final value that is paid to eBay as part of the listing fees.

Final Value. The final bid on an auction; the amount for which the item sells.

Fixed-Price Listing. An auction that has a predetermined price on one or more items; there is no bidding and works the same way as the Buy It Now feature.

Flat Shipping Rate. A set shipping rate that a seller charges for an item no matter where the buyer lives.

Foot Traffic. In retailing, the people walking by or into a store.

Gallery Picture. For a small fee, sellers can add a thumbnail picture to their auctions that will appear next to the item title in search results.

Gift Services. An eBay service that allows you to feature your item as a gift and let buyers know that you offer services such as gift wrapping, cards, and shipping directly to the recipient.

HTML. Stands for Hyper Text Markup Language, a simple language used to create web pages which can also be used to enhance eBay listings.

ID Verify. Establishes proof of identity for sellers and buyers on eBay.

Indefinite Suspension. The suspension of a user's eBay privileges for more than 60 days with no definite reinstatement date.

Insertion Fee. The nonrefundable fee charged by eBay to post a listing; fees vary by type of listing.

Live Auctions. A way to bid real-time at offline auctions through eBay.

Maximum Bid. The maximum amount that a buyer is willing to bid and pay for an auction item.

Minimum Bid. The lowest amount that can be entered as a bid for a specific auction.

Multiple Item Auction. *See* Dutch auction.

My eBay. A section on eBay that shows all of a member's activity, including sales, purchases, watched items, favorites, account activity, and more.

New Item. Items listed within the preceding 24 hours are considered new and are automatically marked with a rising sun icon, which is removed when the listing is more than 24 hours old.

Nonpaying Bidder. A bidder who wins auctions but then does not pay; eBay has strict policies for dealing with nonpaying bidders.

Password. A data string used to verify the identity of a user.

PayPal. eBay's online payment service that allows sellers to accept credit card and bank account payments from buyers.

PowerSeller. An eBay designation for experienced, reputable eBay sellers who consistently sell a significant volume of items, maintain a 98 percent positive feedback rating, and provide a high level of service; PowerSellers are marked with icons next to their user IDs.

Private Auction. On eBay, a type of auction where the bidders' e-mail addresses are not disclosed on the item screen or the bidding history screen.

Reserve Price Auction. An auction that has a reserve price; buyers are not shown the reserve price, and sellers are not obligated to sell if the reserve price is not met.

Reserve Price. A hidden minimum amount the seller is willing to accept for an item listed for auction.

Second Chance Offer. Offering a nonwinning bidder a chance to purchase your item.

Shill Bidding. The deliberate placing of bids to artificially raise the price of an item; shill bidding is not allowed on eBay and is illegal in many jurisdictions.

Shilling. An old auction term that means using phony bids to inflate prices.

Sniping. Placing a bid in the closing minutes or seconds of an auction.

Spam. Unsolicited commercial e-mail.

Spoof E-mail or Phishing. An e-mail that appears to be from eBay or PayPal asking for personal or financial information (often asking the recipient to verify their eBay or PayPal password); users are advised not to respond to these e-mails and to forward them to either spoof@ebay.com or spoof@paypal.com.

Starting Price. The price at which bidding on your auction begins; also, the lowest price you are willing to accept unless you have specified a reserve price.

Supplier. A company that sells goods and services to other companies.

Trading Assistant/Trading Post. An experienced eBay seller who sells items on eBay for other people on consignment; the physical location where a Trading Assistant operates his or her business.

Traditional Auction. An auction where a seller lists one or more items with a starting price; buyers are able to bid on the auction until it ends with the highest bidder winning.

Turbo Lister. An eBay tool that allows sellers to create and upload bulk auction listings instead of manually entering information for each auction.

Unpaid Item. When a buyer commits to buy but does not follow through with payment.

User ID. The name by which you are known on eBay.

Vendor. Another term for supplier.

Want It Now. A place on eBay where buyers can post requests for items they are looking for; sellers can respond with matching eBay listings

Wholesale. The sale of goods in large quantities, usually for resale.

Index